JUST BELIEVE

JACK'S INSPIRATIONAL TRUE STORY TOLD THROUGH HIS MOTHERS EYES

TARINA MARCINKOWSKI

JUST BELIEVE

Jack's Inspirational True Story Told

Through His Mothers Eyes

Disclaimer:

The events within this book are based on a true story, written by the author. It is told through her eyes explaining her private thoughts, emotions and opinions, and in no way, should be taken as medical or health advice.

The names of medical institutions, hospitals, doctors, nurses, medical staff, and other characters have been changed within this book to protect privacy. Any names of family and friends that have not been changed have been agreed upon through a written agreement allowing original names and events to be used.

ISBN: E-Book - 978-0-6486855-0-0

ISBN: Paperback - 978-0-6486855-1-7

This book is dedicated to a beautiful and enlightened soul... my son Jack. His light shines upon the world, healing it with love. The messages of truth that he brings continue to show us that life is about being who we truly are and nothing else. I am proud to call you my son, as I am proud to be your mother. I love you unconditionally.

IN GRATITUDE

· ♥ · ♥ · ♥ · ♥ · ♥ ·

To the loves of my life, Anthony and Luke. There has never been a moment when I did not acknowledge how blessed I am to have you in my life. The love and support that you give me have kept me going and continues to shine upon my soul every single day. I am truly grateful.

To my parents and Anthony's parents, we thank you for your continual love and support that has never wavered all the days of our lives. We love you.

To all of our family and friends who have been there for us, you are always in our thoughts and prayers. We are blessed to have you.

Thank you, Uncle Colin, for always coming to our aid when we call.

To Sarah, my endless treasure trove of knowledge and support, there are no words to thank such an amazing soul. To Jenny, there is never a moment good or bad that we don't end up in laughter and tears. I thank you with all my heart for that. To Kezza, for teaching me to embrace life's moments when I am thrown out of my comfort zone. To Joey and Kate, thank you for just loving Jack as you continuously do, unconditionally.

To all the doctors, nurses, and hospital staff we encountered within this journey who shone their light upon us, many of you were our angels just when we needed you. I thank God that you were part of our lives even for just a moment.

To our Nansie, you are loved so much. Thank you for your heart of gold.

INTRODUCTION

· ♥ · ♥ · ♥ · ♥ · ♥ ·

The beginning seems so long ago, and there is so much to tell you. I want you to know everything, and I mean everything, no matter how good or bad it may seem. This will be Jack's story the way I saw it as his mother, and it will be my tool to remember our journey for the rest of my life so that I will never forget.

I sit and wonder what people will think of me. Those who will be angry or upset by what I will say and what I will not say. Some will be hurt because they didn't realise how much they hurt me or impacted me with the things they did or said. I have learned so much. I have become at peace with my life in this world, with you, and with God.

This book was never going to be written, I told myself, for many different reasons that you will understand along the way. Now I have realised that I need you to know exactly what Jack went through, what I went through, what we as a family and friends went through, and of course what you could possibly go through one day yourself. This is my point of view, my truth, through my eyes as a mother. That is all I can give you... my truth.

Will you be angry? You who are a family member, a friend, a nurse, a doctor who is reading this right now? Whoever you are, if I offend or anger you, I am truly sorry, for this is not my intention. It is time for everyone to know this journey, one unlike any other. This is the story of my beautiful son Jack, how I saw it, my thoughts and my feelings, and that is all.

Why am I writing this now? There have been so many stories in the past to tell. Why is this one so different? You will see why I have chosen to write this book. It is the only way I know how to help or comfort others. How can I possibly ignore those other mothers and fathers and beautiful little children who right now are dealing with the same things my family has endured? How can I do nothing? How can I do nothing while they sit where I used to sit? This is all that I know I can do for you: tell the truth with no lies. The journey we have gone through will be shared.

It was not good enough to go through what we did with such intensity, as if to emphasise an unbearable capacity of pain. It was not completely right... not in my eyes. But time has a way of healing wounds. You will see a journey that shows you how even when people have hurt you, love truly is the only way. I believe that all of us do the best we can with the knowledge we have at the time... even me.

My job through this book is to tell you a story that is not uncommon in the world today, and to give you an understanding that there are people around us who need our love and support without judgement, no matter who they are. I wish to inspire you with the knowledge that even when things seem unbearable, anything is possible. All you need to do is... Just Believe.

I send you love.

CHAPTER 1

When it comes to the devastations of this world, I am brought to tears by the natural reactions of human beings. They stand together no matter what and do everything necessary to survive, rebuild, and start again. Normal people try to save lives without thinking twice about the danger to themselves. They become one. I am so proud of our kind. But what would make me prouder is if we did this every day, without the need for devastation to prove what we can do for each other. What is truly important, every day, is to love one another.

It was Jack's second birthday, and Anthony (Jack's dad) and I had almost cancelled the party because of Jack's vomiting. He had been ill that morning but eventually came good. A few days before, the doctor had diagnosed him with an ear infection. He was put on antibiotics for a week, but he was still a little vomity and wonky on his feet, but that was understandable. It was also July in Australia and winter time, the time for colds and flus.

What a beautiful boy Jack was, he was growing up so fast. I felt guilty because I'd returned to work at my previous employer in retail and managed to get myself stuck in their quicksand. I had gone from just one or two shifts per fortnight about six months ago, which was perfect for me, to four or five shifts per week.

"We need you!" they said. "There's nobody else who can do it!"

My poor mother was taking care of Jack more and more, which was unfair, as she was not working because of an injury. I had started feeling like I was neglecting Jack as a mother. How was I going to tell my employers that it had all become too much? I felt guilty if I didn't do the work. Who else would do it? And, of course, we needed the money.

We had planned a Hi-5 party for Jack's birthday with his friends; he loved Hi-5 so much. Jack was a beautiful boy with golden blonde hair and green eyes, just like mine. His ability to bounce a ball consecutively without any sign of losing his rhythm was a sure sign that he would be good at sports. He had a strange run to him though, kicking his legs out to the side while he moved, but that probably was due to him being one of those kids who tended to W-sit with his legs. You know, bum on the ground and legs bent to the side.

Ouch! (Though I must admit, I too still sit like that sometimes.)

We were all having a great time at the party, especially Jack. There were games, cake, presents and lots of fun with his much-loved balls to bounce. This was a relief after such a hard morning. All the kids were enjoying themselves, but every now and then, Jack would just fall over. It was quite lucky that he didn't hurt himself badly.

I did a little research in a few toddler books about balance and unsteadiness. I found that for kids it was normal to become preoccupied with what they are doing and can accidentally walk into things or lose balance at times. They are still learning to keep their feet on the ground.

I was put at ease, and with Jack on the antibiotics, it all appeared to add up.

Jack had always been a vomity child. Not a full-on reflux baby or anything like that, but enough for me to call out a doctor when he was only about two months old. The doctor said the flap on babies' stomachs tends to be a little floppy and not yet matured, so sometimes the milk comes back up like a little spill. Jack wasn't doing projectile vomiting; he was just spilling. The problem was that his spilling seemed to be in large quantities all the time.

Jack had all his check-ups and vaccinations like he was meant to have, or should I say, like we are all told to do. I had decided to have all his check-ups with the same paediatrician from when he was born, just to be extra cautious. So, when he turned eighteen months, we reported to the doctor as always. My main concern at this particular check-up was his eating. He was still on mushy foods and choking or vomiting on things like bananas and biscuits. His favourite frog shaped chocolates were eaten easily, though.

The paediatrician did a complete check on Jack, including his throat, because of my concern. He found everything to be normal. He told me it was probably behavioural and that some kids do it for attention. He knew Jack well, because he was the one who was there during Jack's birth.

Jack was a week late at his birth and weighed in at only five pounds three and a half ounces. I had so much blood taken, and tests done to find out why Jack was so small. Even though Jack started life a little rough, he was always strong; he was always okay. After starting out in a humid crib for around a week, he fed normally and continued to grow.

Just before Jack was born, my obstetrician had gone on holidays for a few weeks. I will call her Dr. L. I was quite late into my pregnancy and I was worried that she would not be back in time for the birth. At this stage in the pregnancy you have weekly appointments with your doctor who measure you. When I went to the consulting obstetrician, he measured me for the two weeks she was away and was quite happy with my progress. When Dr.

L. returned, she was concerned that the baby had not grown at all in her absence.

"Sometimes doctors measure a little differently from each other," she told me.

She sent me straight down for an ultrasound to find out the measurements of the baby and to see if all was going to plan. They were pretty much right on the mark, with five pounds three ounces as the weight. Though it seemed that all was well with the baby during the ultrasound, it was planned that I would return that night at midnight and be induced.

Five seconds after I was induced, I was on oxygen, having massive contractions, and feeling the need to vomit. The baby was stressed, so I was zoomed down for an emergency C-section. And then there was beautiful Jack. He was the first grandson in all our families and the first great-grandson for Anthony's grandmother, who was already a great-grandmother to three girls.

After all that had happened in the hospital, we returned home. I attended my follow-up appointment for Jack with the paediatrician a few weeks later. He seemed to think that Jack had a big head compared to the rest of his body. Jack was sent to have an ultrasound on the soft triangular part of the skull (anterior fontanel) to see if there were any problems. Anthony was away at the time, so Nansie (my mum) came with me, thank God. You just need that extra support sometimes. The scan showed there was nothing out of the norm.

The doctor said, "He must be all brains!"

I agreed.

At the eighteen-month check-up with the paediatrician, my Jack did nothing but scream. I mean screaming, red-faced, in tears! The paediatrician looked a little puzzled, as if to suggest that Jack's reaction to the check-up was not normal. But Jack was a clingy kid, and he was not accepting of many males. I wasn't concerned about it, but I was completely embarrassed.

The final thing we had to do at this eighteen-month check was to look carefully at Jack's walking. Jack and I left holding hands, but the doctor wanted to see him walk by himself.

"Just let go of his hand for me so I can see him walk on his own," the paediatrician instructed.

As I did so, another doctor in the practice distracted him, he had heard the commotion from next door.

"What are you doing to that poor kid?" he asked.

Our doctor's attention was pulled away from Jack and his walking. By the time he returned his gaze to us, Jack had grabbed my hand again because he was so upset. I looked at the paediatrician as if to ask, "Well?"

"Yeah, that's all good," he said. So, we left.

I was worried that the paediatrician hadn't paid enough attention to Jack's walking, but it didn't seem to be a big thing. He was the doctor, and he knew what he was doing, right?

Now here we were, two years old, injections up to date, all checked over, and growing up fast. Too fast! What a cool Hi-5 birthday party. We all had a fantastic day.

On the Wednesday after Jack's birthday party, I decided Jack could need another dose of antibiotics because he was still uneasy on his feet. I took him back to the family doctor's surgery but saw another doctor, as our original doctor was unavailable. We had seen this particular doctor a few times before in the past, so we were happy with that. She checked Jack over.

"He's fine. There is no sign of an ear infection at all."

I sat there for a short moment, looking at her. Then I asked, "Then why is he so unsteady all the time? If there is nothing at all wrong with him, why is he like this?"

She watched Jack for a little while, and as always, he appeared to be a little wobbly, but not as bad as I had seen him that morning.

"Well, he seems a little unbalanced to me, but fine. If you're still worried about him after a few days, bring him back in to see us on Friday," she suggested.

The next day, Jack's vomiting had become bad. It was mainly in the morning after getting him up or after a bottle of milk. Nansie was so upset with seeing him this way that she suggested we take him to the southern hospital not far from where we lived to get some advice. I just thought that maybe he had something wrong with his inner ear, an infection further in that the doctor couldn't see. We agreed to take him to the hospital just in case.

The gentleman at the desk listened to our concerns and agreed that it probably was some sort of ear infection. He asked us to sit down and wait our turn. He also gave us a red liquid for Jack to drink from a syringe, it was for dehydration. We told him that Jack wouldn't drink it, but he asked us to try. So, we did. Jack never took paracetamol well, it always ended up in vomiting. We tried so hard to persevere with the red liquid, but we only managed to get a small amount into him. He was upset and refusing to cooperate.

People went in, people went out. More people arrived and went in, and then they came out. We were there all day continually asking when it would be our turn.

"It won't be much longer," the man at the front desk would say. I know Jack didn't seem to be much of a priority, but it was becoming a little unfair.

Finally, it was our turn, and we went through. A doctor listened to our concerns and checked Jack over and once again found absolutely nothing wrong with him. The hospital would arrange for a paediatrician appointment on Monday with one of their own paediatricians. The other option was for Jack to have a CT scan of his brain as soon as possible. We were then told that the side effects of CT scans could possibly include brain problems or even brain tumours.

Come on people are you serious?

If Jack has a CT scan and nothing is wrong, I have still agreed to give him one. This scan could possibly cause him a small amount of learning disabilities or maybe start up a brain tumour.

I started to cry. No one could give me an answer as to what to do. They all looked so bewildered, unable to help. We got up and left. We would wait to go and see the paediatrician on Monday.

The very next day, Nansie and Poppie (my dad) came around. Nansie was crying after Jack had just vomited again.

Maybe he was allergic to milk?

It was his comfort, but it had now, especially in the mornings, became the thing that was making him ill. I rang my local doctor's surgery to book an appointment with the same doctor we had seen on Wednesday, just as she had told me to do.

"Come back on Friday if he gets any worse," she had said to me, but to my surprise the secretary informed me, "I'm sorry, but she does not consult on a Friday."

"Are you joking?" I said. "She specifically told me to come back and see her today, and she doesn't even work on Fridays?"

I then rang Jack's paediatrician to get an emergency appointment with him, and guess what the receptionist said to me?

"I'm sorry, but your doctor has moved his practice interstate for the next two years."

What the ...? Thanks for the notice!

"Could you book me in to see the other acting paediatrician as an emergency please? I really need to see someone desperately!" I asked her.

"I'm sorry but you'll need a referral from your local GP to see that particular paediatrician," the receptionist told me. I started to cry on the phone to her. It was all becoming too much.

"I need someone professional to look at my son immediately," I told her through tears. "My local doctor is not working today, and now my paediatrician has left the state, so what do I do? Please help me!"

And with no care or thought to anything I had just said, she replied with a firm voice, "You will just have to take him to the hospital."

Wow. There was nothing much left in me then, and so I answered her, "I've already done that too! Thanks for nothing!" I hung up the phone. I sat there telling myself,

All right, think. What should I do? Do I wait until Monday for the appointment that the local hospital made for us, or do I try again with another hospital?

"What about the specialist hospital in the city?" Nansie asked me. I decided that I would ring and speak to someone first. A lovely gentleman answered the phone, and I explained my concerns to him.

"I definitely think that you need to come in and see one of the doctor's here," he answered. He was so sure, so definite. It was the first time I felt like it was the right thing to do. So, we went.

CHAPTER 2

*We have all done it. You've done it. I've done it. I will own up
and confess that I have done it many times. I have allowed my
mind to judge wrongly. I have judged people, places, moments
and experiences in a negative way, and for what? So that my
ego could be right! Well...not anymore! This is what shuts the
door to living life to the fullest. What if that person, place,
moment or experience was exactly what I needed, what I had
been looking for all my life? I wouldn't know because I shut it
down before I could even see what joy it could have brought to
my life.*

We went through to emergency, and there were so many people
there. Sick kids vomiting and screaming. I thought that we would
be there waiting forever, but it was about half an hour later that we were

called in. I explained Jack's symptoms once again to a female doctor, and after hearing it all she conversed with another doctor.

The verdict was that he would need a CT scan. If the CT scan showed nothing at all, then we would have to give Jack an MRI. A CT scan uses radiation, while an MRI uses magnets. After all we had been through, I thought I would prefer Jack to have an MRI.

"Why can't you just give him an MRI first instead of having to do both?" I asked.

The reason was that with only one MRI machine, and of course politics involved, this is the way they did it. So be it. The female doctor decided to get another doctor to have a chat to us about everything, so we would feel more comfortable.

His name was Dr. Abe, and there was only one question he needed to answer for me, "If this was your child, your son, would you do this?"

With confidence and his eyes on mine, he said, "Yes, of course! This needs to be done." He explained everything to us clearly.

We had dealt with so many doctors in the last few days. All of them, every single one of them, was from a different cultural background. The ones at the southern hospital and now at this hospital. When Dr. Abe walked in, he too was of a different cultural background, and to be honest, I actually began to get angry when I first saw him. I don't know why, I just did. I never saw myself as thinking badly of others because they were of different cultures, but I suppose I'd just had enough.

The thing, though, is that when he spoke and looked at me, it was different from all the others. He spoke with confidence, and he spoke with compassion. He spoke like a man who knew what he was doing. He spoke the way I needed someone to speak to me, just like I thought a doctor should do, with insight and knowledge that I didn't have. It wasn't the doctor's cultural background or what the doctor looked like; it was about the confidence he had in presenting his opinion. I was wrong to judge him because of my past experiences, I apologise, and I will never do it again. He was the help I had been looking so hard to find for so long.

Anthony arrived at the hospital, and Nansie and Poppie left. While we waited, surprisingly, we were told that because we had ticked to come in as private patients, the public doctor wouldn't do the CT scan. Instead another doctor would do an MRI at six o'clock for us. What a relief! Something had worked out in our favour.

I felt like we were in a position we could move on from. Let's have the MRI, find out that Jack is fine and continue with our lives. Poor little Jack hadn't had much to eat all day, but he fell asleep when the female doctor came back in to give us the paperwork and discuss a few things.

One of those things, to my shock, was that if they found nothing wrong with Jack, he would not be returning home with us.

Pardon me?

Well, not until they found an explanation for his symptoms. Wow! I know they have his best interest at heart, but so do I. You think you're in control of your life and decisions made for your child, but really, you're not. I felt like a pawn. But right now, I needed them, I had to play by their rules. I had no choice.

I had never needed a doctor in this way before, or a hospital. I believed that they knew what they were doing. They had studied and trained for years, and so they knew more than I, surely. Didn't they?

The time came, and Jack was put under the anaesthetic. It was tough especially on Anthony, because he had to hold Jack, as it had been recommended for me not to as I was pregnant. Anthony held Jack while they spread strawberry scent over the gas mask, which made it easier to put it over Jack's face. When Jack fell asleep, Anthony laid him down onto the bed where we had to leave our poor little baby, heavy and motionless. It was a strange way to see him. Heartbreaking!

We left the MRI area and went to the cafeteria to get some dinner, a hot dog each. It really wasn't going down well, and we both stopped eating after a couple of mouthfuls. It's true what they say about hospital food. Then a private number rang on Anthony's mobile, which we missed. We saw that a message had been left.

"It could have been the doctor!" Anthony said.

We left our food and began running back towards the MRI area when Anthony's phone rang again, and sure enough, it was the doctor. We were all alone standing there in the MRI waiting room. Where was everyone? Anthony started the conversation with, "We're here out the front of the MRI!" and then his face was just devastated listening to what the doctor was saying to him.

"What? What?" I asked. I was thinking it couldn't be bad, no way. Jack is fine, he just has to be.

Anthony hung up the phone, looked at me, and said, "He's got a brain tumour!"

I remember just standing there thinking, *Don't play games with me. This doesn't happen to us. Someone is just playing a huge trick on us.* I felt like I was on a TV show or something. Where were the cameras? We hugged each other, and we both just cried and cried.

"It can't be!" I said. "We are good people; this doesn't happen to us!"

I had never experienced anyone in my family or friends' families or husband's family who had ever been hit with such a massive heartache. We were all normal, so why now? Why us? Why did we have to be the ones with this cross to bear? It did not feel real. I was a Catholic girl who was always good and believed we would be watched over lovingly by God forever. This had to be a mistake.

The doctor came through the MRI doors, and he just walked straight up to me and hugged me. We had not met this doctor before, but because Dr. Abe had gone home for the day, we had Dr. Post, who was now on duty. Dr. Post was very kind and loving, and he pulled us aside into a room to discuss things further.

The room was a large disabled toilet. Dr. Post pulled up a small waste paper bin, turned it upside down, and sat on it. Anthony stood while I sat on the closed lid of the toilet. The doctor was very sympathetic, but to be honest, I really don't remember much of what he said. He told us that it was in the cerebellum part of Jack's brain, which confirmed the symptoms of being off-balance and vomiting.

We watched from the doorway as they slowly rolled Jack past us on his way to recovery. We stopped them, so we could both give him a kiss. My poor little baby, so many tubes and cords hanging out of him once again, just like when he was born. I just wanted to hold him and let him know that it was going to be okay, but I couldn't.

That poor kid. He must have been in so much pain, and I had yelled at him sometimes because of his vomiting, because we had been told that it was behavioural. I thought he was being a bad boy, but instead he was just in so much pain that it was all too much for him. How do you say sorry for that? What a horrible mother. How do you take it back?

Anthony rang both of our mothers. My God, how did he do that? How were we even breathing? I had never seen my husband so upset. The tears were endless.

Thoughts raced through my head: *It can't be true. It always seems to be us. Why? It will be all right, everything will be fine, God is just testing us, and we will be fine.* I wanted to be sick to take the pressure away from my body.

It had only been a few weeks ago when I had said to myself, "You know what? I am really happy!" I had jinxed myself. It was my own fault. Why had I said such a thing? Why? "I am truly happy!" Now look at us. Happy was only for a moment and now our future looked grim.

Somehow, we made our way back up to a designated ward, where both of our parents were waiting for us. I was surprised that they had made it to the hospital so quickly. What a moment. There's nothing to say, really. We were exhausted and angry—at God, at everyone. How could this be?

This hospital made me remember an accident that had happened about twenty-two months ago to my niece Lauren. She was two years old at the time. Lauren was Anthony's brother Brenton's eldest daughter. A group of us had ordered some drinks at a café one afternoon at a busy shopping centre; two of them were hot coffees. When the lady served them to the table, she placed the hot drinks too close to Lauren and her little eight-month-old sister, Ashley. Lauren ended up with third degree burns to her right foot and ankle after one of the hot coffees fell down into the boot she was wearing.

Lauren had to have skin grafts to try to fix it up, and it left a scar. She was in the burns ward at this specialist hospital after it happened. I was angry that my God had allowed such terrible suffering for a little child, and now to my Jack.

God, how could you do this to such a beautiful child, so helpless?

I knew what everyone would think when they found out about Jack. I knew because I thought exactly the same thing when I watched little Lauren screaming while the emergency service people were helping her with her burns. Her mother, Kerry, held her tight after doing all the right things and acting so quickly when it happened. I turned my head, so I didn't have to look at them, because I couldn't stand to see the child in pain anymore.

I remember thinking, *Thank God it isn't Jack! Thank God it isn't him! He is here in his pram. It could have so easily been him. Thank you, Lord, that it wasn't my baby boy! Thank you for protecting him!*

Where was Jack's protection now from you, oh mighty God? You allowed a little girl to be burned and scarred for life, and now you allow a beautiful two-year-old boy, my son, to have a brain tumour. Numb. I felt just numb.

We were then moved to a four-shared room in the same ward but away from the burns area awaiting Jack to return from recovery, which was hard. You have a massive amount of information to deal with, and then you must deal with that information with three other strangers in the same room watching on. We were devastated that we did not get a private room.

I know it sounds lame, but the smallest things are sometimes the hardest. When you have such news in your life, believe me when I say that all you want to do is lock yourself up into a little room to just sit and think. It's like you need time to work it all out and realise what to do next and to even imagine it's not real.

Jack returned from recovery, and he lay sleeping in a big single hospital bed. He looked so small in such a big bed. He had always slept in a cot.

From that moment, he turned from my little baby boy into a big strong boy.

CHAPTER 3

The light always shines brighter in the darkness. You will appreciate people more when they have stepped into the darkness with you, holding your hand. They are the ones who decided to bring along the torch. In those dark times their help has made it easier for you to see because they have shone their light for you.

We were told that Jack had been booked in for brain surgery on Sunday morning at eight thirty. I wasn't sure if I was glad that they knew what to do to go about fixing him or angry that we were just told and not asked, consulted, or given other recommendations. We were just told that they would be giving him a brain operation. No one asked.

No one sat down with us and said, "Hey, is it okay if we slice your kid's skull open?"

Were there no other options?

Anthony went home to collect some belongings that we would need while we stayed at the hospital. In his absence, I found myself suddenly being taken into a private room with a social worker to discuss my feelings. I told my mum, Nansie, that she was to sit in with me to be a witness, and she did.

What's the point of discussing my feelings now? I haven't even been able to comprehend what the hell is going on.

Wait! There's that feeling again of not being in control of my life. The social worker and I sat across from each other while Nansie stood behind me.

I looked into the social worker's eyes and thought, *So, lady, do you really want to know what I think? How I feel? Trust me you don't!*

She spoke quietly and asked me a whole bunch of questions, gently waiting for an answer for each one. I answered them. I answered them the exact way I knew she wanted me to answer them. She appeared happy at how strong and understanding of the situation I was. Little did she know that I was just moving this process along, so I could get back to Jack and my own private thinking process.

She explained to me all the emotions I might feel now and, in the future. She looked at the net of support in my life that were my family and friends. I was calm and convincing and extremely easy with her.

I looked deep into her eyes and, once again, thought, *Do you really want to know what I am thinking?* What I was thinking in my head went a little like this:

Don't just sit there, lady, and psychoanalyse me! Telling me how I should feel. You have no comprehension or understanding of the situation I am being tragically faced with. You do not know me, and don't think that just because you have studied the human brain and people's reactions in different situations for X amount of years that you can simply place me into a certain category. Oh wait, did you even study? Oh no! Not to be rude or anything, but fuck off, lady, and let me be with my sick little boy.

The interview was successfully over quite quickly because I played the game instead of poking her eyeball out with a pencil like I wanted to do. Phew! I'm glad I got that off my chest.

Man, I sound like a bitch, but some people just think that their way is the best way. "This is how we do things around here, it's proven," and they do these procedures just as if reading off a list. I'm not a freaking list, people! I am a human being. Treat me like one instead of a number. Otherwise, don't waste my precious time! So, obviously anger is a natural reaction.

Oops, think I lost it a bit there with the social worker thing, but remember, this is the truth of how I felt. What can I say? Would I be the only one who thought this way? I don't think so.

My brother Shane and his wife, Kerry, came in to see us. We were all just so speechless. Jack had only six months ago been the page boy in their wedding, and now he lay asleep in a hospital bed unaware of how sick he really was. For a moment, I felt strange, hot and sweaty and unable to breathe and then it went away as quickly as it had come.

The night passed slowly by, and that feeling of uneasiness continued to come and go, more rapidly each time. It made it hard to even try to sleep. Everyone else left, and the nurses allowed Anthony and I to stay the night after such an emotional day. Apparently, it wasn't normally allowed to have two people stay overnight because of occupational health and safety rules; only one parent could stay. I would have loved to have seen them try to make one of us leave. Anthony lay on the bed with Jack while I had the fold-out stretcher bed. How could we sleep anyway?

It hit about eleven o'clock, and that feeling of nausea that had started out quite small a few hours earlier now had me sitting up and rocking myself at the end of the bed. I had to get up; I felt so sick. I went to the toilet, the one a little further away so no one could hear me, and I vomited. I had never felt so sick. I honestly thought it was the half a hot dog I had eaten previously, because it didn't go down well when I ate it. I ended up after the fourth or fifth time of vomiting telling the nurse at the desk that she would have to change one of the bins in the toilet.

She looked at me sideways, asked me a few questions, smiled, and the next thing I knew I was being escorted down to the women's emergency section of the hospital for observation. I must have looked bad. They were all very lovely, I must admit, very sympathetic to me with what I was going through. I was put onto a drip and continued to vomit the night through. I was a little nervous, because I was three months pregnant. I was worried about the baby.

The following morning, a lovely obstetrician came in and did an ultrasound on the baby and found everything normal. She even gave me my first photo! You could see that the baby had its little tongue sticking out. I had a small smile and then tears once again.

Poppie had to pick me up around ten that morning and take me home. They didn't want me to see Jack in case I had a contagious virus, and he needed to have his operation desperately. My poor little baby! All I wanted to do was give him a cuddle. I didn't even get to see him wake up.

I remember the slow drive home with Poppie, bowl in my hand. Anthony rang on my mobile. He was so upset, desperate for me to be by his side. He had just had the neurosurgeon and accompanying doctors come and speak to him about the brain surgery. They had told him all the things that could happen to Jack through having this procedure. Things like having to learn to walk again, needing a shunt if the brain fluids didn't flow correctly, speech impediments, eye problems, and facial paralysis. Anthony was so upset, and I was just crying. I was being taken home away from the two people who meant the most to me in the entire world. What could I do? I had never felt so ill.

When we got home, I continued vomiting. I had reached an all-time record in my life. There couldn't possibly be anything left, and then...

Oh shit! Was that blood coming up?

It was now noon, and I rang the hospital straight away to inform them about the blood in my vomit. I was told to come back to the woman's section of the hospital for more observation. I felt a sense of relief about that, because I would be closer to my boys.

At this time, my friends Wendy and Sarah had rung, and they had decided that they would come and pick me up and take me back to the hospital. They just wanted to come and see me after hearing the bad news about Jack. I was a little anxious, because I wasn't sure how I would react to seeing them for the first time since the news. Over the phone, each conversation was different. Wendy was strong and in control, and Sarah a complete mess. I suppose Wendy was trying hard to be a supportive friend, yet Sarah could not hold in her sadness. They were so very different, that's what I loved about them.

I had a quick shower, and before I knew it there was a knock at the door. I took a deep breath and opened it. Wendy hugged me tight straight away, and Sarah completely lost the plot and hugged me blubbering. It was so strange. For the first time, I did not cry. It is a moment I will never forget. I just didn't cry, and I don't know why. Usually if someone so much as sheds a tear, I will well up and fight back the tears, but at that moment it was like I was empty. There was nothing left. I was just … numb. It was like a body mechanism that kicks in when you need it, to allow yourself to cope and continue.

Sarah apologised. "I told myself I wouldn't be a mess with you, I'm sorry!" she said.

Why on earth was she apologising? She was crying because my little baby boy was suffering, because my entire family was in pain, and she was apologising for it. What a sausage! We all deal with things differently, and it made me a little more secure with our friendship. It was because my pain had become hers, and she had allowed herself to just be herself. That is a true friend, honest.

Wendy drove us all to the hospital, and she tried to take it easy as I held the bowl, praying that I wouldn't have to ask her to pull over. Thankfully, I didn't. When we arrived, I was placed straight into a room in the woman's section. Nansie came in, so did Brenton and Kerry, who I was seeing for the first time since we got the bad news. Sarah's husband, Andy, turned up there too.

The nurse questioned me and seemed to think that I was all right, that it was just bile coming up and not blood.

"When was the last time you vomited?" the nurse asked me.

"At twelve o'clock," I said. "Will I be able to see my son? They said that they would prefer it if I didn't in case I was contagious, and with him having his operation tomorrow ..."

"Let me check," the nurse said.

It was all looking quite positive, and when she returned, she agreed happily, saying, "Yes, that's fine. It's been over twelve hours since you have vomited, so we don't see a problem with you being able to see your son."

My heart dropped as I looked at her. "The last time I vomited was at twelve o'clock a half an hour ago, not twelve o'clock yesterday."

"Oh!" she said with an *oh no!* look on her face. "Let me just ring the ward again and have a chat with them."

She left once again. Thankfully the nurse in the ward where Jack was staying felt positive about me coming up to see him and agreed that I was fine to be with him. I was so happy, and up we all went. I was greeted by a wonderful nurse who was called big Martha, whom I instantly loved. She hugged me tight, and I soon realised that she had been the one who had agreed to let me see Jack.

"This happens sometimes when we get bad news, our bodies just react," she said. "You'll be fine, go and give your boy a cuddle." I was teary, and I thanked her. She was so kind. She was just such a wonderful person.

I discovered that they had moved Jack into a twin-share room, and Jack was the only one in it at the moment. We realised that it was the burns unit of the ward, and the rooms were not being used. It was a little eerie, as this was the unit Lauren was in after her accident. It was so nice, though, to have the room to ourselves to just be together.

There he was, my little baby. He had his bottle of milk, which was his comfort, and he sat on my lap. I held him tight in my arms, and I kissed and rubbed my nose into his hair. I loved doing that.

I could see that he had gotten a great deal worse. The operation was scheduled for the next day, and there were moments when I wondered how we could wait that long. Jack was enjoying his bottle, until he vomited it everywhere, all over the floor, all over me. He was now getting in a bad way. It was hard for him to keep anything down. He had to be fasted from midnight. Sucking on his bottle was the only thing that gave him comfort, the only thing that made him feel better, even though it was making him vomit. It was going to be a long, hard night.

Anthony's parents, Ma and Pa, took Jack into the toy room, where Jack tried his hardest to play. They stood by his side; he had become so unbalanced on his feet, he couldn't even be left or just watched, he had to be supported otherwise he would fall over.

My cousin Sharlene and her husband, Paul, brought in pizza for all of us to eat, which was really nice. We did not eat in front of Jack but waited until he fell asleep. Soon everyone left after giving Jack kisses on the head. None of us knew how Jack would be after the operation the next day. How scary it was to think about it.

Anthony and I took turns sleeping with Jack on his bed, because he didn't want to be by himself. There was another hospital bed in the room which we snuck onto as well, so Anthony and I could both get some sleep.

We got through most of the night well until the early morning. At about six a.m. Jack started to cry for his bottle. We tried everything to distract him, but he was crying so loudly in this ever-so-quiet hospital. Poor Jack. His cries echoed throughout the hallways even with the door closed. The only thing that gave him peace, a small distraction from the pain, we were taking away from him. Thankfully, they decided to bring his operation forward, and soon it was time for us to go in.

Oh God, this is it! We were allowing these perfect strangers to cut open our beautiful son's perfect head ... my sick son's beautiful head. How could I possibly describe how hard it was to hand him over to them? Watching Jack go under the anaesthetic was hard once again, his body slowly getting heavy in Anthony's arms. Jack then gracefully fell asleep.

The anaesthetist said, "Don't worry, he's in good hands, we'll take good care of him." It was reassuring, but he was still a stranger.

Anthony lifted Jack onto the hospital bed. We held each other crying as they wheeled him away, and we let him go.

CHAPTER 4

Happiness is not earned, nor is it something that we need to strive for in our lives. It is something that is owned by each and every one of us. It is a choice. If you cannot be happy right now, you will never be happy thinking that way. Strive for your dreams so that they can create a joy that with this happiness you already own is an unbelievable and unique fulfilment in life.

How long it was! Forever even. It was a massive operation, waiting, waiting, and waiting. You think terrible things even though you know it's supposed to be a five-hour operation and it's only been three.

You still think, *why is it taking so long? Has something gone wrong?*

There were so many of us in the room, friends and family, just waiting. I wasn't sure if I was anxious about Jack finally getting out of that operation or if I was afraid of what they were going to tell me after they had completed it. It was all of it that had my stomach in knots. I just wanted him to be well again. All back to normal. Why couldn't I have that?

I can, I can have that! I thought. *My beautiful Jack, a great kid!*

Once again, the thought of being a good Catholic person hit me, and of course Jack was going to come out of the operation with none of the possible defects they had predicted would happen. We were good people who did the right thing, all would be well.

Stay positive and anything could happen, I told myself. *He will be exactly the same but better. He will be well again.*

I needed to refresh myself, so I would feel better after how sick I had felt previously. Wendy's husband, Jason, ended up going down to the hospital's kiosk and buying me a brush and some moisturiser, which was very helpful. I couldn't be bothered going to get anything myself, and it was an opportunity for him to help in some way. Everyone felt so helpless. They wanted to help us, but what could they do but just be there?

After a long hot shower at the hospital I felt like a new person. Food was still a little bit of a no-no for my tummy, but I was feeling a lot better. Anthony and I lay on the extra hospital bed in the room and tried to get some kind of rest while we continued to wait and wait.

Time passed by slowly. Eventually we were told to make our way to the ICU (intensive care unit) where Jack would spend the next night. When we arrived, we were told that they would need some time to prep Jack before we went in to see him. The neurosurgeon who had just finished Jack's operation spoke to us about how it had all gone. We stood in the doorway while our families stayed back and gave us our privacy.

Holy shit! What was he going to say?

You can't read these doctors; they always look so emotionless. My thoughts were running wild as he began to speak to us about how the surgery had gone.

"The operation went well," he began, "or as well as we could have hoped."

What does that mean? Good? Bad? What?

"Jack lost a bit of blood, and we did need to give him a blood transfusion during the operation."

Oh my God! A blood transfusion, that can't be good! What about Ma? What is she going to say and think? She is a Jehovah's Witness, and they don't believe in blood transfusions! Wait, Tarina! Stop! Focus and just listen, all that stuff doesn't matter!

"We got about 90 per cent of the tumour out," the neurosurgeon continued.

My mind kept on freaking out, *What do you mean 90 per cent? That means there is still some in there! What happens if it grows back?*

"We left a thin layer like a sheet of paper," he explained, "because it was just too close to everything, and we would have caused some brain complications. We will have to wait and see if there are any other side effects to the operation, like facial and speech problems. The tumour was about 2.5 centimetres in size."

What? That is massive! Could you imagine a ball 2.5 centimetres in a little child's brain? That's like a 5-centimetre tumour in an adult's brain, which is just incomprehensible! No wonder that poor kid was vomiting! My God!

I thought again of the times when Jack became overly emotional and ended up vomiting, and I would get mad because I thought it was behavioural, because that is what the professionals had told me. What a terrible mother! How could I bear to know that I had allowed him to suffer while I got frustrated with him for not wanting to go to bed or because he was clingy and wingy for no reason? Hello! Big reason! He was in agony! He had the headache of the century!

"Jack will have to undergo chemotherapy and radiotherapy treatment after his recovery, and we'll see how we go from there," the surgeon went on.

Chemotherapy and radiotherapy! No! I don't want him to have to go through all that!

"So, is it malignant?" I asked.

He shook his head and said, "We don't talk malignant with brain tumours. There are four different types of brain tumours, and there is one that is a benign tumour, and the other three are more serious. I do believe that the tumour Jack had was a type that could possibly grow back. It is called a medulloblastoma, but we will have to send it in to be tested to be more certain about it. This is why we follow it up with a good program of chemotherapy and radiation."

So, in plain terms, it's bloody malignant! Why can't they just say it? No, no, no, no, no!

"What about other people?" Anthony asked. "Have they survived this?"

"Yes, of course!" the neurosurgeon said confidently.

"How long have they lived for?" I asked.

"There are adults well into their thirties who have had this operation as children who are fine now and leading normal lives," the neurosurgeon replied.

"We were told that you couldn't have radiation until you were three years of age. How will Jack be able to have that?" I asked.

"He must have some sort of radiotherapy, but that will be up to your oncologist, and what they decide will be the best way for you guys to go," the neurosurgeon told us.

"What would have happened if we didn't find his tumour?" I asked.

He looked at us and said, "I suspect that he would have haemorrhaged sometime within the next twelve months."

So that was that! They were ready for us to see Jack now, but what did I think about the conversation with the neurosurgeon? I think I felt like it didn't go as well as I had planned it would. Why was everything going wrong? I was being positive, and I was a good person, so could I get a break here or what?

It appeared like my poor little Jack had a great deal more left on his plate. Why couldn't it have been a benign tumour? I didn't understand how this could all be happening to us!

Oh God, you are so great ... yeah, when you want to be! Where's your fantastic power now, oh great one? Good Catholic girl. What a bunch of shit!

I was so afraid to go and see Jack. What would he look like after brain surgery? I just wanted him to look like Jack, to just be my beautiful Jack, that's all. Anthony and I went through to the ICU, and the nurse showed us into the cubicle where he was. He had a nurse at the end of his bed at a desk monitoring him. He was lying on his side, peacefully asleep. He looked beautiful as always, and he looked just like Jack. It was a small relief to see him. His face was normal from what I could see, no paralysis.

He had a very long bandage that went from the middle of his head all the way down to a little bit past his shoulders. The nurse let us know that the bandage they put on him was a lot bigger than the incision, thank goodness. They didn't have smaller ones at the time, so they put on a larger one. I'm glad that she told me.

Jack moved a little in the bed. I bent down close to his face looking at him and said, "Hello, baby."

Jack softly said, "Mummy ..."

Wow! He spoke! If only I could tell you how much joy there was in my heart, to know that he could talk after they had told us he might not. How wonderful! What a brave kid. Others from the family went to see him, and I was over the moon knowing that he could talk and that he still looked like my Jack.

Anthony and I took it in shifts during the night to be by Jack's side. We had been assigned a room just outside of the ICU area where there was a bed and a bathroom. It gave us an opportunity to rest during the night. I think we took it in two or three-hour shifts. It was a very long night, but I must admit that the nurses who took care of him were fantastic, very professional. I felt comfortable there, and I felt that Jack was safe. It was easy for me to forgive the paracetamol overdose that occurred while he was in the ICU, that I later found out about.

Every now and then Jack would move around a little, but not much, and every so often they would turn him. When it was Anthony's shift, Jack called out for his bottle, so with the permission of the nurse Anthony gave it to him. Within moments, Jack had vomited it up all over the bed, the nurse changed the sheets. This male nurse did not flinch at the thought of having to clean it up, and he appreciated Anthony's help.

These are the people in our world who make a difference. This man loved his job and told you so no matter what task was at hand. He was peaceful, and this is what you need when you are suffering. Although it's his job, he knew only to put Jack's and our best interests first. Wherever you are now, we thank you for being so kind.

CHAPTER 5

Some days the hill that you are climbing feels like a mountain. Each day it becomes steeper, the air becomes thinner, and your fears grow stronger. But with faith you will realise that you never had to climb the mountain in the first place because all you had to do was move it. Kaboom!

T he night passed, and morning came, which meant a visit from numerous doctors who had come in to look at Jack. His doctor, Dr. Post, the one who found the tumour in the MRI, said that it looked like Jack had facial paralysis on the right side of his face.

No! But his face looked fine!

This could slowly heal itself in time, but in many cases, it was permanent. Maybe I couldn't tell because Jack hadn't done much more than sleep.

There was hope that it would heal and return, so we both stuck with the hope that it would. That's all we had, so that's what we did.

Another group of doctors came in. They were from the ophthalmology department, and they were concerned with Jack's eyes. I remember them quite clearly, because it was like a wave of people trying to all fit into this small cubicle to see and hear what the doctor in charge, who was very short and blunt, had to say.

She waltzed in and began her spiel. "Yes, it looks as though he has facial paralysis on the right side, which means he will need drops in his right eye because he will have trouble blinking and keeping that eye moist. The left eye has turned inwards, like a lazy eye would, so he will need some patching done as soon as we can. This is due to being face-down in surgery for so long, and ..."

I looked at her in dismay and was trying to get some sort of a question out, but I found that I was stuck. All that was left was a small kind of "Um ..."

She saw that I was overwhelmed and just stopped and said, "Don't worry, we will fix it."

That was that. Before I knew it, she and the rest of her crew were gone, like a whirlwind. Poof! It just left you with a whole bunch of whys, really. Obviously, the surgery got very close to everything, because things weren't looking so rosy.

Wasn't Jack going to look like my Jack anymore?

The last thing I heard her say was, "Don't worry, we will fix it!" so I held onto that thought and left it in her hands, whoever she was.

That afternoon, we found ourselves waiting to give Jack a CT scan to see if the fluids in his brain were draining correctly. If they weren't, Jack would need a shunt inserted into his brain surgically. Just another little thing to be worried about, along with the fact that I had a fear of CT scans.

We had during all this time met a little fellow named Ian who was a part of the team with the neurosurgeons. He had been wonderful so far. He was like the right-hand man of the neurosurgeon, and he was full of information. We were never scared to ask him any questions at all; he was carefree and easy to get along with.

Ian was running around like a headless chook while we all waited for Jack to go into his CT scan. He was looking a little anxious, I thought, maybe because things weren't going to plan, and no one was sure of what was going on. He then returned and told us that the MRI machine was free and that we were going to give Jack an MRI instead.

Hooray! I thought.

Wow, this dude knew how to get things done. I was really pleased that we had Ian on our team.

The MRI showed that the fluids were slowly draining correctly, and the tumour was no longer showing up. (A tumour has to grow to half a centimetre before it can even be picked up by the MRI machine.) The good news was that the fluids were doing what they were meant to be doing.

We were then placed back into the same ward where we had initially come from, but further down into a four-shared room. This was difficult once again, especially because we were put in with two young noisy boys. One was about four and one was about seven, and they were screaming and yelling all day long. The two boys had been in the hospital for months, and it had become like home to them. Sadly, one had been injured through a car accident and the other I wasn't sure how he sustained his injuries. These boys ran a complete and utter muck. The nurses tried to contain them, but they were not there to be parents, and the parents needed to go to work to survive.

The hospital had different people attending to the boys throughout the day. Sometimes they would have physiotherapy or go and do some craft activities, which gave us a break. For the rest of the day, they would run around screaming while half the nurses tried to chase them and settle them down. One nurse tried her very best to be like a super-nanny to them. She was good, but man, they were full on! No need to buy these guys trampolines. They were using the beds!

The problem for me wasn't that they were there just being kids, because it wasn't their fault that they had been there for so long and bored out of their minds. The problem was that Jack had just had brain surgery, and as one nurse told us, every little tiny sound, even us whispering to him, would aggravate him. He was on painkillers and other drugs, which helped. What didn't help was the constant noise.

There were so many times that we asked for a single room or a room with fewer patients, but they refused us each time, telling us that the single rooms were for children who had viruses or illnesses that were contagious. Which of course was understandable. To our shock, the little boy who was in emergency with us who had fallen out of bed and hurt his eye had a lovely single room, and yet my son, Jack, who had just had massive brain surgery, was placed in a shared room with two boys who loved to have fun.

I know that I didn't know all the information about the boy who injured his eye, but I did know that I spoke to that lovely family and knew that the little boy had fallen out of bed. I didn't know how serious he was; he did leave within a few days. The other factor was that Jack had the bed right next to the nurse's desk, so that he could be continuously monitored. It just breaks your heart to watch your son in such agony, knowing that it's the noise that is hurting him and you can't do a freaking thing about it.

One of the boys' parents had come in that evening and stayed a whole of about fifteen minutes. It was like the kid had overdosed on his daily intake of red cordial. The parent couldn't deal with it and left. The stress, you could see it in them. They had jobs and other children, and it appeared to be too much for them to cope with. I felt sorry for the little boy. He didn't ask to be here, but I could understand how much pressure the parents were under. Why couldn't things be better for all of us?

CHAPTER 6

There are times when the people we love the most, our friends and family, can become the thorn in our side. If you can understand that a thorn grows from a rose, a magnificent flower, in order to protect it then you will know that a room always smells better when they are in it.

That day, we had a small, plump little lady who introduced herself to us as our new social worker. Her name was Samantha. She did not stay long, and she told us that she would return to see how we were doing regularly. My last run-in with a social worker had me nearly jumping out of my skin and wanting to tear the woman's head off. Maybe that was just bad timing.

In some strange way, I was thinking, *Where's the other lady I spoke to the other day?*

I had an attachment to her now that she had dealt with me before. Even though I was not in the best of moods when speaking to her that first time, I found that I wanted her instead of someone new. Weird, isn't it?

Nansie came to the hospital late that afternoon and told us that she was going to stay the night with Jack so that we could both go home later and have a proper sleep. It would be hard to leave Jack. I knew that he was in the best hands ever with Nansie.

Anthony slowly picked up Jack and held him, which is what we had been taking it in turns to do. This wasn't the easiest of jobs because Jack had cords all over him, one being the IV in his foot that had given him a little trouble. They were giving him all his medication through this. It did make things easier, as Jack never liked to take anything orally.

As Anthony lifted him up, Jack yelled out, and then he pulled his arm up to his chest with his hand bent over forward, just in the same way that people do if they have some form of brain damage.

Nansie let out a shocked, "Oh ..." as if to say that Jack had given us a sure indication that he wasn't right, that he had brain damage in some form.

It couldn't be bad, could it?

He had only just said "Mummy" to me yesterday, but we could not yet know the extent of the damage the operation had caused or how close the tumour was to different parts of his brain. Two and a half centimetres is big, too big.

How do you withhold such emotion? My whole world was crumbling down. Was he going to be in a wheelchair forever? Was he going to be unable to do what normal children do? This was the first time I wanted to be normal again, a normal family with kids who just bump their heads or scrap their knees.

I promise I won't work so hard anymore. I will appreciate Jack just as he deserves. Please just make him normal. I wondered if anyone up there was hearing me.

A lovely nurse started her shift that afternoon and introduced herself as Martha. Another one! Apparently, she was nicknamed Little Martha, and the first one I had met was nicknamed Big Martha. It must be the name. She had a little light and a desk right at Jack's bedside, and she was going to be there all night with both Jack and Nansie. It was great to know that they were both in good hands.

After a small fight with Nansie about her doing the night shift, both Anthony and I agreed to go home and leave her with Jack. We were absolutely exhausted. It was quite difficult, actually. Every time we walked passed Jack's bedroom, it was like a cold breeze blew out of it. It was so cold and lonely without him in it.

Our family and friends were fighting to do things to help us, and a great deal of that was making dinners. It made it easy to just pull already made food out of the fridge or freezer, and it was one less thing we had to worry about. We each had a long hot shower then sat by the TV for a while to chill out. I don't really know if we were relaxing or if we just didn't know what to do with ourselves, we went to bed and tried to sleep.

The next morning, we went back into the hospital early. Little Martha was about to go home for the day. She told us that Nansie had not slept a wink.

"I kept telling her to sleep on the fold-out, but she refused!" Little Martha said.

That's Nansie for you. Jack had slept on Nansie in the big recliner chair for most of the night. It would have been uncomfortable, but Jack was settled, which was the most important thing. He had kept insisting on a bottle, which Nansie watered right down and had not had too many repercussions. Everything went well for the night. Nansie went home for a much-deserved rest.

During that morning, while Jack slept on me, Dr. Abe our original emergency doctor came in to see us. As soon as I saw him, I began to cry.

"How are you all? I thought I would come and see how you are all doing." He held my hand, and I thanked him for being so lovely and being that one person who, in our time of need, was there for Jack and for us.

"I'm sorry, but because my shift finished before Jack had his initial MRI, Dr. Post is now your doctor."

"That's fine, he's very lovely too," I said.

"So, the operation sounded like it went well, and I hear he's going to need a bit of chemotherapy?"

"Yes, he will," I said sadly. We spoke together for a few moments after that, which was nice.

"Well, I better be off. I just wanted to see how you all were after hearing the results. Best wishes to you all, and I hope everything goes well for you."

"Thank you once again for making us do what was necessary to find out why Jack was sick."

"It's my pleasure," he said as he grabbed my hand once again and then left. He was an inspiration to me. I had been so stubborn and frustrated with the whole system, and because he was calm and open with me, he had started the ball rolling for my Jack to be well again. He had showed me that I was never to judge the look of someone. We as human beings have no right to judge each other's looks or mistakes. We are all made the same, and we are all loved the same. We don't outrank each other in any way. Not to God.

All God wants us to do is to live by his love. He gave us his commandments to follow, to do what is good. He is the only one with the right to judge us. So, remember, even though it's hard, do what's right and fight for its survival. Don't just judge without knowing the truth. I have learned a big lesson, and I admit it. I am not afraid to show my humanness, for this is how I learn.

We struggled through another day. Today we met Heather, who was from a children's cancer charity. She was extremely lovely.

I remember having a chat with her and thinking stupidly, *I don't know why this lady has come to see us, because Jack doesn't have cancer! He just needed a tumour removed, and he is going to be fine now. Oh my God, the C-word ... cancer. Jack doesn't have cancer, does he? I hadn't even thought about it like that. Things are quite bad, aren't they?*

Heather gave us a big tractor for Jack to play with, a bag of information, and a stuffed toy dog, which was the mascot for the charity. It was really nice of her to bring so much. She was genuine. Heather left when all the doctors came to see Jack for the day, and I thanked her as she left.

Nansie had returned for another night shift with Jack, but Jack's bandage had started showing signs of stuff oozing onto it. The nurses weren't sure if it was just the wound or if his brain fluids were leaking out. *Pardon? Brain fluids leaking out?*

The acting ward's doctor thought it would be fine but told the nurses to change the bandage over. Jack become upset when one of the nurses started to get ready to change it. Now, the nurse who was taking care of Jack at that time was one we had encountered before, and she was not one we had taken a fancy to. She was quite rough and tended to just laugh a little if she did something wrong, as if to take away the humiliation of it. Instead it just made her look incompetent. I will call her Nurse M, she was very tall and dark-haired, with thick black glasses.

She was prepared to change Jack's bandage with her tray of instruments that she had organised, and she pulled the curtain a little way around to get some privacy. Everyone could still see us, so basically that did nothing.

Then it began.

Anthony held Jack while Nurse M tried to wipe over the edges of the bandage with a solution. This was to help the bandage come away from Jack's skin without pulling or tearing. Jack just screamed and screamed as we all tried so desperately to console him. The nurse fluffed around here and there as if she couldn't do it, and she seemed as if it was just too much for her to do. It took me all I had in me not to beat the living daylights out of her giggling little face! Eventually the bandage got removed. At last, she was capable enough to take it off.

There it was, the confronting incision that was supposed to be not as big as the bandage. It was massive! It started halfway down his skull and went down his neck and past the start of his spine. It was the most terrifying and horrible thing I had ever seen. No parent should ever, ever see such a thing! Jack was screaming, and as he turned his head from side to side, this clear fluid would run out of the wound about three quarters of the way down. I just cried. I couldn't take it anymore!

My God, you are so cruel! He is a baby! Why do you continue to do this to him? To us!

Nurse M cut a piece of gauze. When she went to measure it, she realised that she had cut it too small. We had to sit there for another ten minutes watching while she did it all over again. She ripped open a brand-new gauze, got the tweezers, got the scissors, oops it slipped, try again. The stress had mounted to the greatest I had ever felt. I was going to rip it out of her hands and do it myself. The air in the room was thick with the tension from all of us just staring at her, our eyes piercing her every move. Nurse M must have felt the glares, she was shaking slightly.

All I thought was, *Ask for help if you need it. Why embarrass yourself or continue this absolute agony for everyone? Just ask for help!*

Everyone around was looking at us, the nurses' station, the other kids, anyone who was near at the time. It was a mess! At that moment, Little Martha came in to help. She had just walked in and started her shift for the night. Hallelujah! I trusted her. I was so relieved. She must have seen all the commotion, and she knew just by looking at us that we were in distress, and so she took charge.

Little Martha told Nurse M what to do and assisted her, so she would do it right. Nurse M cleaned the wound and redressed it, and even though the dressing wouldn't stick down correctly onto Jack's skin, it was good enough. Anthony and I were being told through this distressing process to go home, because it was almost ten thirty at night and the car park closed at eleven.

"No!" I insisted. "I am not leaving until I know that Jack is settled and that he is in good hands!" There was no way in the world I was going to leave while that woman was anywhere near my son!

Finally, the job was done, and Nurse M left for the day. Jack settled into bed, and Little Martha set up her desk and light at the end of Jack's bed once again.

"You had better go!" said Little Martha.

"Go!" Nansie insisted.

It was now almost eleven, and with peace inside, I knew they were all in control once again.

"Thank you so much. You have no idea how much you have helped us," I told Little Martha.

"It's fine," she said. "It wasn't hard to tell you guys needed some help."

The thing was that she was the only one out of everyone watching us who did anything about it. She gave us a wonderful smile, and so Anthony and I both left quickly and made it in time to get the car out of the car park.

Oh God, could you imagine if it had closed? It would have been just another thing to deal with. It was costly enough to park in the bloody thing all day, let alone having to pay for it to be there overnight or pay to have them come and get the car out for us. We had purchased a weekly ticket, which was mildly cheaper than normal. We were unsure of how long it would be until we all would return home, before Jack would come home. Once again, we drove home for the night.

CHAPTER 7

Just as the sunsets at night and rises the next day, we to do the same thing. As we close our eyes to sleep, we let go of the woes from the past. As we open them the next morning we welcome a new beginning. Yesterday has passed, embrace today!

After another night of staring into Jack's empty room and about a thousand tears, we returned early the next morning, even before seven o'clock. The two troupers, Nansie and Little Martha, were just fine. They had worked together to make sure all went smoothly throughout the night. Little Martha was a gem, and Nansie too of course. Jack lay asleep, and we were all able to have a coffee and some toast before he woke.

The ward had a parent's room where you could sit and have a coffee and make yourself some toast. It was a significant room, because in these times, it was very important to take breaks to unload the stress and just take a moment for you. There was a fridge and a TV, and it would become our own little peace haven, even for just a moment during the day.

Jack looked so peaceful, the poor little child. How was he even coping? It was hard enough to watch him, but to *be* him. He was just so small. How was he so brave? It was now time for the doctors to do their morning bed calls, and in they came, about eight of them at a time. The neurosurgeon had been informed that Jack had oozing fluids on his dressing and that when he moved his head it would cause the oozing to become worse.

"Let's see it!" said the neurosurgeon.

Ian was there too, and as Anthony held Jack, they swiftly took off a small amount of bandage and back on it went. Just like that, quick and painless.

"Yep, that needs to be redone, book him in!" He turned to us and explained that the brain fluids were leaking through the wound and that Jack needed to go back into surgery to have the wound restitched to fix it up.

Are you serious? Anything else? Shit...is there anything else?

"It won't take long at all," the doctor concluded, "but it needs to be fixed." And then, poof! He was gone, and so were all his clan, except Ian. Ian stayed to start the process of Jack going back into surgery to have the leakage fixed. Anthony and I had questions, and Ian stood there and answered them all.

We were informed that Jack would go under anaesthetic around two thirty that afternoon, which meant he had to fast. Not that he was eating much, just lots of custard, but it meant once again trying to explain to Jack why he couldn't have his bottle. Before any anaesthetic, you have to fast. It is dangerous if you have any food in your stomach, in case of vomiting, especially if you have tubes down your throat.

Here we go again!

Jack had to undergo another procedure. I must admit, where the wound was leaking from was right where you turn your neck and it twisted; you could see the skin tightly pulling. We were getting ready for another hard morning of trying to keep Jack occupied and his mind off of his bottle.

Surprisingly something went our way. There was an opening at 11 a.m. Jack was able to go and have his procedure done earlier. He hadn't eaten much that morning anyway, so the fasting time was all fine as well. It all worked out.

Hooray!

While Jack was in his operation, one of the nurses asked us if we would like to move to another shared room within the same ward, because the two boys we were sharing with were so lively.

"That would be great!" I said relieved.

We packed up our gear, and we were taken further down the hall to where we had the back-left corner of another four-room shared space. It was a little more private, and the kids were a lot less noisy.

We got comfortable, put all our gear away, and waited for Jack to come back from the operation. In the meantime, we stuck up photos of Jack and some cards and drawings his friends had done for him. It brightened up the space we had.

It wasn't long before Jack returned, just as they said. When Jack did return, the IV in his foot, which had been irritating him, had been removed and another one had been put into his left arm. Hopefully this one would give him less grief. Although they had now put it in a bad spot, as Jack's right side had become weaker than his left from the operation, which meant the IV would restrict his good arm.

I remember sitting there while the curtains were closed overhearing the couple with their daughter next to us discussing the situation they were in with their doctor. The brief of it was that the little girl had a stick wedged into her eye after falling over at the playground. No one was quite sure whether it would be all right or if she would lose the sight or the eye completely. I was devastated. I could hear them desperately asking all these questions about what they could do. Things like stem cell were asked about.

I was so sad for them, but in the midst of it all, I thought that if God had come down and allowed me to swap my situation with theirs, I wouldn't have even hesitated. It was a terrible thing for them to be going through but give me a deal and I would have taken it.

Another day passed with us trying to find ways to entertain Jack. Nansie returned after she had slept through the day and decided to stay overnight again, which was a massive help to us. It was better when you could actually get some sort of rest for the day. For Nansie, the numerous years of night duty for nursing helped her get through these nights. So once again, we went home to sleep.

We returned early the next morning to the hospital, but this time we did not have such a good reception from Nansie. Usually we would have some breakfast before Jack woke up, but this morning, she was upset. She desperately needed to go home and shower, as Jack had vomited all over her, not that she cared about that. It was the way she had been treated throughout the night that made her, and us, quite angry.

We had moved rooms, so our favourite nurse Little Martha was no longer Jack's nurse. It had been quite early in the night when Jack woke like he had done every night and wanted a bottle, which was fine. He ended up laying on Nansie, which he had done every night, but he vomited on Nansie and the floor.

She buzzed for the nurse to get some help because Jack wanted to stay laying on her, but she needed to clean it up because the smell was horrible. It took so long for someone to come. Eventually a blonde nurse came in who Nansie had never seen before. Nansie explained to her what had happened. The nurse had just come in to give Jack some medication through his IV, and she did that without saying much of anything. Having done the job, she went to leave.

"Excuse me," Nansie stopped the nurse. "Can you please watch Jack while I clean myself up? I have vomit all over my clothes."

The nurse agreed unenthusiastically, as if it was an inconvenience for her. Nansie went to the bathroom and washed herself, barely taking two minutes. She quickly wiped over the floor, too. Once again Jack ended up back on her lap, but this time Nansie put a towel underneath him.

There was no help at all for the whole night, and Nansie battled with Jack and his bottle, having to somehow get him a bottle while he still wanted to lay on her. She managed somehow. Whenever she asked for help, all she received was attitude. In the end Nansie decided that she would do it alone and ignore that the nurses were even there.

We could see how exhausted she was. She had sat in that recliner smelling like vomit for about seven hours with Jack laying on her for most of the night. Nansie was amazed by the lack of care and kindness that was present that whole night compared to the last two nights. They made us all feel so unimportant.

I know it's hard. It must be to do such a job, especially night duty. Doing the same thing every day, watching children get hurt and slowly recover, from small things to bigger things. Maybe you become numb to it all so that you can get through each day till it's time for you to go home until the next shift. Then you do it all over again.

Where is that human natural instinct to just be kind, to help someone out beyond all the other stresses that seem to build up in your own world, to be nice or even just smile? Is it too hard to put yourself in other people's situations? Is it easier to not care? I suppose then you don't have to worry.

Is it not the reason we live, to show people compassion, kindness, and love? Remember this as you read it: one day when you're having a bad day, or you just don't feel like cracking a smile, you may have just made someone's life a little harder, a little more unbearable, from just a small act and such a small moment in time. Be aware that you have played a part in a situation that may have been completely different if you just could have been a little nicer. Amazing, isn't it?

Nansie went home to clean herself up and have a much-earned rest. She never gets upset, but they must have really pissed her off. She probably didn't tell us everything either.

That day at the hospital was a nightmare! Jack was screaming uncontrollably; there was nothing Anthony and I could do to console him. This behaviour went on all day. We were pushed to our absolute limits, and no one knew what to do to help us. Jack must have been in agonising pain.

He had already had all the painkillers he could have, but he was hitting and kicking and screaming in such a way it was unbearable to watch. His little face was twisted like an animal in pain.

The left side of his face scrunched up, and yet the right side had no movement at all due to his facial paralysis. He showed his teeth only on the one side. It was the first time I had really seen how much his facial paralysis was affecting him. His right eye was so wide open I thought it was going to just pop out because he had no facial strength to even blink his eye correctly. It was only a half blink, so most of the time it stayed open. He had no movement and no control on that side of his face, and he had no expression, just nothing.

His beautiful little face was terrifying while he was screaming. What could we do? Nothing. Just hold him and watch him go through this. The pain doctors who came around every morning started him on MS Contin for pain relief, which is morphine. His IV morphine was slowly weaned and finalised.

His paracetamol went through the IV, which was so much easier, but he continued to scream and scream. The social worker Samantha decided to pop in to check on us while Jack was practically jumping out of Anthony's arms.

"Is this a bad time?" she asked.

Are you freaking blind? My mind screamed at her.

"Yes, it's a bad time!" I said as I turned my back to her and just started to cry. That was enough. No more people! Unless you can stop my little boy from this attack, then don't come near us.

She placed her hand tightly on my shoulder and said, "Be strong! It's okay!" Then she left, and for some reason what she said helped me. It brought me relief.

Jack continued like this for the whole day. I had never felt so useless in all of my life. It was like having my heart crushed all over again. We took Jack for a small walk around in a pram, and when we returned he finally lay on the bed and slept. Anthony slept on the bed with him, cuddling him, while I sat in the recliner and fell asleep too. We were all exhausted.

The day was nearly through, and I felt such guilt for the other three people sharing the room, having to listen to us for over nine hours of screaming. After having to share a room with two overexcited boys and not being happy about it, to now have Jack being the one who was making all the noise made me feel terrible for the others. I just don't understand why we couldn't have been put somewhere more private. It wasn't the removal of tonsils, it wasn't a broken arm. It was brain surgery on a two-year-old child.

The nurses wanted to try patching his right eye because his left eye had become lazy because of the operation. His good-seeing eye, the right eye, needed cream to lubricate it because he couldn't blink properly on that side because of his facial paralysis. The eye that was affected, the left, he could blink and keep moist, but it was not functioning correctly. Jack would have been having a doubled vision effect, because his left eye was slightly turned in. If they didn't patch the right eye, forcing the left to work harder and getting the muscles working again in the left eye, then the brain could possibly shut the eye down completely.

We didn't want Jack to lose vision in any eye, but the problem was that today was not the day. Jack just ripped the eyepatch off with no hesitation, screaming again. Would you want your good eye completely covered, leaving you with poor uncontrolled vision, and while you were already having a really bad day? I don't think so! That was enough for the day, and we decided that we would try again tomorrow.

One of our friends had brought in a packet of balloons. To see the last of this horrible afternoon out, Anthony had a great idea to blow them up and let them go. We had the curtains closed all around us, so when we released the balloons, they would hit the curtain and fall to the ground. We tried to catch most of them, because the idea of them falling to the ground and then having to blow them up again was quite a gross thought. The floor was terrible, and a quick wipe over every second day by the cleaners didn't cut it in the cleanliness department for me.

Jack calmed down quite a great deal and would begin to laugh from the noise of the balloons being released. We did this for as long as it took to keep

Jack entertained and happy. How wonderful it was to see him laughing. This had been the longest day ever.

CHAPTER 8

*Stop! Look! Listen! Each moment deserves your attention.
From the smallest miracles like butterflies and bees flying
through the sky, breathing clean air, taking a long hot shower,
playing with your children, eating chocolate, hugging your
parents or buying something you have saved up for. Everything
deserves a moment to see the beauty that it holds within it.*

Jack was irritable with Nansie again throughout the night but comparing it to the previous night he was much better. The nursing staff were more accommodating and professional except when Nansie had to stop the nurse from putting Jack's daily eye cream in the wrong eye. Not that the eye cream would have caused any problems, but after telling her three times, Nansie ended up pointing to his right eye so that she got it right. The nurse had been standing in front of Jack like a mirror image and finally realised her mistake. She must have been thinking it was the same right as her right, but it wasn't.

Jack was still vomiting every day because of the pressure and swelling from the operation trying to heal itself. The tumour had been on the point in his brain where it would cause vomiting. It was expected that Jack would be upset, the poor little thing. He had so much to deal with, and it just seemed to keep on mounting up on him. We were told that his behaviour was quite normal and that it was just a process we had to ride out.

Even trying to get him to take his medication was a chore, and the doctors wanted his IV in his arm removed, which would mean that any medication he needed he would have to swallow. He was having MS Contin every morning and night, and today it was quite an eye-opener when the nurse came straight in and handed the MS Contin over to me.

"You can give it to him," she said.

I backed off and put my hands up and said, "No thanks, I don't want to give it to him!"

It always ended up in either screaming or vomiting. I'm no nurse, and I didn't want to be. The drug doctors came in for the morning run, and they were great.

The main woman announced, "I'll give it to him!"

She picked Jack up in her arms, sat on the chair, and slowly made him suck it down, with his disapproval, of course, but she did it. Little did I realise that I would soon be the one who would have to give him all of his medication when we were finally allowed home.

Jack's physiotherapy was being stepped up along with his occupational therapy and speech therapy. His speech was not a concern, but it was great to go because the speech therapist, Jess, was so lovely. All of them were wonderful, but she just had that spark about her. Jack took a shine to her, because he never caused a scene during her sessions. He just did as she said, and he enjoyed it. He was fine sitting on a chair, and he was speaking as he did before the operation. It just got better and better, with him starting to put three words together.

When we returned to the hospital room after his therapy sessions, I hadn't realised how bad Jack's balance was. I had gotten on the floor with him to play for something different to do. I sat him on his knees as he had always done in the past, and he just slowly fell forward. I gasped and went to grab him quickly, but I couldn't get him in time. He ended up hitting his forehead on the ground. He was screaming. My heart was breaking.

"I'm so sorry, baby!" I yelled devastated.

I felt so horrible. What if I had caused more trouble to his brain? Oh my God! I held him tightly as an egg came out where he had hit his forehead. I started to tear up. I felt so bad that I had caused him more pain on top of all the other pain he was having.

The physiotherapist and OT girls ended up getting Jack a large soft, thick mat to put on the floor of the hospital room after I told them what I had done. It was an extra bonus, seeing as the floor always appeared to be so dirty. Now we could cover it up and it would be safe for Jack.

We would take Jack out for different appointments within the hospital, including physiotherapy and OT, which on many occasions the girls did together. It was Jack's coordination and walking that needed the most attention, because we had to teach him all over again. It was frustrating to him; he knew that he used to be able to do it, and now he couldn't. For me, the hardest thing was trying to hold him while he wanted so much to walk. But he just couldn't do it. He used to throw right-handed, but now he did everything with his left, because he had lost a great deal of coordination on his right side.

His left-hand throw was so fast and hard we would laugh. We would put Jack in his lock-in high chair from home with its seat belt and attached tray, and in his hospital room we would get him to throw Play-Doh balls, and man, did they go! He slowly learnt to coordinate his hands to feed himself, which was frustrating at first. He was still on the mushy foods just in case he choked.

Jack was starting to very slowly get better, and by the end of each day he was more often up than down. Some of our friends and family would visit, and each one had to have a turn blowing up a balloon and letting

Jack release it. I think everyone who came in went home dizzy, but we all had fun. Each visit we had was different and kept Jack entertained and happy for a moment. It was another moment that Anthony and I could just breathe. Just a moment each time, and that's how you go on.

The most frustrating part of the day was when we tried to patch Jack's eye. His doctors wanted him to have it on for at least a couple of hours. The nurse who was on for the afternoon was our beloved Nurse M, the one who had caused us so much grief over the changing of Jack's dressing.

Great! This should be good, I thought.

She got a patch and taped it over Jack's eye, and of course he screamed and ripped it off. Once again, she tried, and once again Jack screamed and ripped it off. I had no idea how this was going to work; it was just going to keep on happening.

Finally, she turned to me and said, "Well, I'm going to have to inform his doctor that he is refusing to have his eyepatch on, so the only other option is that we may have to restrain him."

I looked at her sideways and slowly analysed what she had just said to me. *Wait a minute, there it is: she wants to tie Jack's hands to his bed, so he will wear his eyepatch!*

"What?" I said to her.

"We might have to choose to restrain him to the bed," she repeated.

I looked at her like she was some kind of leader in a prison camp and kindly said, "Um, no! I don't think so!"

Was she some kind of psycho? I'm not sure if I was overreacting, but I think that restraining a child to a bed is against the law! The thought of Jack, two years old, screaming and kicking and tied to a bed with an eyepatch on reminded me of movies like *Frankenstein*. Was she insane?

You're a freak, I was screaming in my head, *a freak*!

So, this was not to be an eyepatch day either. Oh well, got to take the good with the bad.

Oh my God, get me out of this hellhole!

The weekend came, it had been a full week in the hospital. Anthony took over the night-duty role from Nansie so that she could have a break and spend some quality time with Jack during the day. At night, I went to her house to sleep for company. Nansie and I got into the hospital very early the next morning so that Anthony could go home and sleep, and we found them both eating away at a packet of triple-coloured wafer biscuits. Jack found them soft and easy to eat.

When Jack wanted a biscuit, he wanted a biscuit. He would scream until he got it, and so he got it. It was so hard to entertain him by yourself, and if he didn't sleep very well through the night, you had to find something to do. The problem was Jack wanting to eat and eat and eat all the wafer biscuits until he would vomit, and that is exactly what he did. The steroid he was on was called dexamethasone, apparently it gave you one hell of an appetite. All Jack wanted to do was eat.

Nansie and I got through another day, that afternoon when Anthony came back in to do the next night shift, he decided to buy a pasty from the cafeteria, and he brought it up to the hospital room to eat it. Jack had not eaten much of the hospital food, not that I blame him. It was still all mushed foods, and the choice was not desirable. When Anthony started to eat the pasty, Jack just looked at him with this stare, he wanted that pasty. Anthony gave him a bite. Jack took the biggest bite I had ever seen, and he chewed and swallowed it. Within a second, he was grabbing Anthony's hands, trying to get the next bite.

"My goodness!" I said.

Both of us were in shock. Neither of us had ever seen Jack eat so well in all his life. Not with solid foods. There is no way that he could have ever eaten that pasty without choking before, and now in a flash he had eaten the whole thing. Gone! It was like a small miracle to us, a milestone to a new beginning.

Jack was getting better. He was feeling better. It was one of the most wonderful and happy moments I can remember in that hospital. We all laughed. It sounds strange, but it was a miracle to us that he was eating normally. Wow ... there's that word normal again. I could only pray that one day it would be true.

CHAPTER 9

Everyone has a story, and everyone makes choices based on those stories. Be brave enough to see the story attached to every person you meet without pouring your judgement over them. If you don't know their story, then don't judge them. Instead understand their story or move on.

The following week passed along very much the same, with physiotherapy, OT, and speech therapy every day to get Jack back on track. The eye people came in to keep checking on him, and we kept trying to patch his eye, we did it slowly and for short periods of time. Jack had calmed down, and so the patching became easier to do. We had the doctors in every morning to tell us he was getting there.

Jack had his bandage removed permanently now, and there it was for me to see every second of every day, that terrible big incision. It became something we would grow accustomed to, some of his hair would cover it. It began to be a part of him. It amazed me that something so horrifying slowly became less intense over time.

He continued to gobble down his food and discovered a love of Toobs (a type of chip). I did hope they wouldn't make him hyperactive, but he just loved them, and we tried desperately to make them last. The last thing we needed was another screaming fit from being hyperactive on artificial colours and flavours!

The only other thing we had to worry about was making sure the brain fluids were continuing to behave and to flow instead of blocking up. If it turned sour then Jack would need a shunt, we definitely didn't need him going through anything more. Ian suggested that Jack wear a tight beanie on his head. This would create pressure against the wound, helping to move the fluids in a good way.

Every day the doctors would come in and check him over, and all seemed to be going well. They squished and pushed around his wound and said that it was all feeling good. When they left one morning, I remember accidentally touching his head around the wound. It was so squishy and soft, not like a head is supposed to feel. It is something I will remember forever. It was weird, like a wet marshmallow, but without the stickiness. It shocked me, I had never felt anything like it.

We walked the hallways of the hospital all day, as Jack hated staying in the little corner of the room we called home. I think we knew just about every nook and cranny of that hospital, and Jack loved it. He couldn't walk, so it was always nice for him to be pushed around.

Whenever we tried to return to the ward, it was so hard. We would get to the doorway, and Jack would start screaming. He never wanted to go back in. Not that I blamed him. It was boring just being in a small confined area.

The hardest thing was to entertain him all the time. We took him to the park outside of the hospital and got him throwing balls around while he was still in the pram. His laugh was so beautiful; although it was different, it was still intoxicating. The sound of it was like the wings of an angel spreading out, a breath of fresh air. It would start you anew after holding so much worry. For just one whole second, we would forget.

Our times of hallway walking were apparently quite the thing to do, as we met up with a young woman who was doing the same with her son, Andrew. We passed each other a few times and finally Anthony stopped to have a chat with her. Andrew was bald, and his head showed a couple of huge scars across it, and he was unable to speak or walk well. He was around the same age as Jack, maybe a little bit older.

The lady told Anthony, as I recall, that Andrew was on play equipment at a park. He was at the top of a slide that was about two metres off the ground, and he fell off, hitting his head. When they got him to the hospital, he had an MRI, which showed a mass of swelling in the brain. He had to have a shunt put in, and now he needed daily physiotherapy and OT and speech therapy. They had basically lived at the ward we were in for a while now, because he needed to attend these appointments every day.

May I say that this woman was so peaceful and never once showed that her son was any sort of burden to her. We saw her many times in our journeys through the hallways and smiled. Deep in my heart, I prayed for her and Andrew, but I found it so hard to talk to her. It was hard enough to know that Jack had been dealt such a terrible card. To hear other stories just made me feel more angry and sad. I silently thought of her as an angel and hoped that they would all be fine one day.

On one of the days we were scheduled to have a play date therapy session with Andrew, which was really nice. The three girls; Jamie from physiotherapy, Jess from speech therapy, and Rachael from OT, organised it for us. The boys played with toys together to help their fine motor skills, like shovelling and pouring and picking up marbles and rolling them down a ramp.

Jack was able to sit at the table or on the floor and concentrate on the task at hand. Andrew was a little different; he had a long way to go to get back to just the basics of sitting, standing, walking, and talking. My heart broke for his parents. Andrew was such a happy child, always smiling and laughing. I would have loved to have seen him before the accident. They were both such brave kids.

Jack had many sessions with each of these girls to get his right side working to its fullest capacity, but he was a little up and down with some of the climbing and mobility tasks, such as walking. He became grumpy quickly, which I think was due to him getting tired easily. Jamie seemed to think that he should be walking by the end of the week, but I thought it was going to be some time yet. Jack's sessions were always scheduled to be an hour long, but most of the time they got cut short because he became frustrated. The days just seemed to be so long.

By the end of this week, Anthony had started to do most of the night shifts while Nansie and I did the days. I sometimes would bring him in a nice takeaway breakfast, which he appreciated, but like most mornings at this time of my pregnancy the toilet always seemed to end up with mine. Damn morning sickness.

One morning, while in the parent's room organising my breakfast, I met a woman whose face looked very familiar. She was one of my customers from my workplace. We talked briefly, and I informed her of my situation and that I would not be returning to work for a while. She was so surprised and sorry for me. Our discussion continued with her son being admitted for a burst appendix after she had vigorously seen doctor upon doctor who told her that he was fine. Now they were here, and she had been so worried about him, especially now that his appendix had burst. They were finally treating him, and she was somehow relieved, even though they weren't out of the woods with it all yet.

I'm glad I acknowledged her and was sorry for her, but how can I explain to you how hard it was to listen to another person's pain and continue with our own as well? It was nice to talk to other people about their situations and to vent my own frustrations and hardships, but once again, I ask you, God, will you come down and change our situation to appendix problems? Not that I hoped that anyone would ever have to go through such a trauma, but if he could just change Jack's to one of the other problems I had heard so far, that would be nice. Scary to say that, but it would.

I suddenly thought about Andrew's mum. Would she have ever thought that about other people? Had she thought that about Jack? I felt like she knew what we were going through, but to be honest, at the time I saw her as being worse off than us. I felt selfish for even thinking that other people's mild problems weren't as important as mine. I would never change places with anyone, because I could never wish this upon anyone else.

There had been a change in the bed next to us, with the little girl with the eye leaving and a new teenage girl coming in who had not let go of her number twos for a very long time. The nurse told her that she was compacted from one end of her bowel to the other. She moaned and groaned for most of the time that she was there, which made me feel better about Jack's whole day of screaming.

Hey God, how about you give Jack constipation instead? Sounds fair to me!

Anthony nearly told the girl to shut up with all her wailing. It seemed that most of the tricks the nurses used on her to fix the problem weren't working. She had refused most of the help. All she wanted to do was eat and drink as much as she could, and all she wanted was chips and Coke. Where do these kids get these attitudes? Man, was I like that as a teenager? I hope not!

She wasn't of small frame either, and it wasn't hard to realise why she was not passing the number twos to the loo. Fruit is good for that, if you choose to eat it. This girl was so young, and already her body was becoming affected and starting to break down. Everything is fair in love and war, though. We had been the noisy ones, and now she had taken over the role. You had to just grin and bear it.

There was a little girl opposite Jack, and she was beautiful, blonde-haired, blue-eyed, and around six years old. Her parents took turns spending the night with her, but they had to leave throughout the day. How sad it was to see so many children left alone. One night, neither one of her parents could stay, and the poor little thing began to cry as soon as her mother left. I went over and cuddled her, we had a chat about the stuff she liked to do, and we read some books together.

"I'm just over there, you know! Just call out to me if you need me, and I will come over and give you a cuddle."

She just smiled and nodded, but every now and then one of us would go over and talk to her. Anthony also went over to her after Nansie and I had gone just to make sure she was coping. When she ended up leaving the hospital, Nansie and I bought her a few presents. She was so excited and happy. Her mother thanked us for taking good care of her, and it was our absolute pleasure.

Anthony's night shifts were always so difficult. One night, Jack slept on his own in the bed, which was fantastic, but Anthony didn't sleep a wink. There was a boy next door in an isolation room who would scream all night, and Anthony could hear everything, even them all talking. The boy's screams were so piercing to him because, as he explained, the child was in agony, just like Jack on that horrible day he screamed from morning to night.

The nurses had to go into this boy every hour, and every time they did, this poor little boy would scream. Anthony awoke sometimes in fear after falling asleep dreaming of this little boy screaming, even when he wasn't. He couldn't quite explain to me how terrible it was, but he compared it to a horror film with someone being stabbed to death. Between the screaming and the constant beeping of machines Anthony was looking like a zombie. How glad I was that I had not been there. Just the thought of it nearly had me in tears. The screaming had not awakened Jack, however, so he had a good night's sleep finally.

We were told that we might have to stay another week. Anthony just cringed with the thought of having to stay in this dungeon for another seven days and nights. Everything was a little unsure at the moment, it would come down to Jack's progress and how happy the doctors were with him.

Jack had another MRI. Only the spine was done, even though it was the head and spine that his oncologist Dr. Marlene had requested. What it showed was that none of the tumour had snapped off and gone down to his spine. He was all clear, which was great news. Jack was meant to have a lumbar puncture as well, which is the procedure to place a needle into his spine, like an epidural but to extract fluids and test them, but this too was forgotten during his MRI.

We had briefly met Dr. Marlene a few days earlier, and she was coming to see us to go over Jack's plan she had put together for the next week onwards, and for his chemotherapy treatment.

When she came to see us, she gave us a written page that she had done herself. It explained some of the things that Jack would have to have done this week coming, and she also gave a brief overview of the chemotherapy treatment. The plan was as follows:

On Monday, which was two days from now, Jack would need to have a GFR (glomerular filtration rate), which was a kidney function check. She explained that he would be at the hospital for quite a while, as it took around five hours to complete.

Dr. Marlene had also booked him in for a lumbar puncture on the same day. This was due to it being missed during the MRI, they had forgotten to do it, and she thought it best to do it all in the same day. She instructed us that Jack would have to fast from eight that morning for the lumbar puncture. That would be hard as the procedure was at two in the afternoon, but he could probably have something to eat straight afterwards. The lumbar puncture required a mild anaesthetic.

On Wednesday, Jack would also need to have an item called a port surgically placed under his skin just under his right nipple. This is what they would use to access every time Jack had chemotherapy. On Thursday, he would need a hearing test. The reasons for the kidney and hearing test was to find out how good they were working before chemotherapy started. Due to chemotherapy having so many side effects, they could monitor any hearing and kidney deterioration throughout this process.

When all was good, and we were ready to roll, we would start a four-cycle chemotherapy treatment, which was around a month each. Followed by a six to eight-week stint of radiotherapy and then about eight months of more chemotherapy after that.

Well holy shit, people! Shall we take a breather? How does anyone do this? This all just seems ridiculous!

I thought it was just chemotherapy, bang, you have it, you lose your hair, and then you're fine. I was so naive, so, so very naive. Was I the only one living with a paper bag on my head? Or are we all just carrying on with our daily lives not really understanding what is going on in the world. Is it because we don't care when it's not happening to us? This was all making me realise what I had been doing my whole life, and that was sleeping!

Wake up! Oh, don't worry I'm awake now!

There were many short-term side effects of chemotherapy that Dr. Marlene discussed with us, such as vomiting and all of Jack's hair falling out. Jack might also become low in his blood counts, which would mean that he would be prone to viruses. Luckily, we were starting all this at the end of winter.

"Does all the kids' hair fall out or do they retain some?" I asked, thinking desperately that I did not want this for Jack.

"All kids are different. Some of them, their hair falls out straight away, some retain a small amount of fluff over their heads. It's all up to that individual."

I wanted to be positive once again, believing that with my faith it would give us some small miracle, like Jack keeping his hair.

"He will also need a nasal gastric tube put down his throat for his oral chemotherapy medication to be administered," Dr. Marlene informed us.

Anything else?

This was just terrible! I didn't understand how it could possibly be so hard! So many things to deal with. It just felt never-ending.

"Can't Jack just orally take the medication?" I asked.

"Older kids tend to take it and have described the etoposide as metallic tasting, but the younger ones don't take it well, and we don't want chemotherapy drugs going everywhere either."

"Do you replace the tube?" Anthony asked her.

"Yes, if Jack can keep it in, we replace it on a regular basis."

"So that means that it can come out?" I asked.

"With the kids vomiting, it does tend to come up. It just has to be replaced every time it does come out. If you're at home and the gastric tube does comes out, you just ring emergency to tell them you are coming in, and they will replace it there. Also, if Jack gets any high temperatures, anything over 38 degrees, you ring the chemotherapy ward and let them know. After a couple of hours, you can monitor him from home, and if paracetamol doesn't work in bringing the temperature down, you ring the ward again and talk to the nurses. They will inform you if you need to go to emergency. It could mean that with his low blood counts, he may have contracted a virus."

It saddens me to think of the beginning. This was the plan, and I felt like a stupid little girl who had absolutely no idea about any of this. It shocked me, and it scared me. I thought chemotherapy was a ray of radiation like radiotherapy, but I was quickly set straight, wasn't I. We are all just sitting in our own little worlds, aren't we? Unaware of the big bad world outside until it secretly decides to come on over and bite you in the arse.

I felt like a child myself. I was thirty-two years of age yet really quite uneducated in this world. It appeared I knew nothing. I had been lost in my own little world that really, now when I think about it, had no meaning until now.

We were told that we could go home the next day, Saturday, which was a great surprise to us. This finalised our fifteen days and nights of utter hell in the hospital. We left with a bag load of medication, which Jack was to take and we as parents had to administer. All we had was a description of how much and when on each packet. The joy of knowing that we would return home was wonderful, but the stress of having to give Jack so many medications each day was unbearable.

One day at a time, I thought to myself. *One moment at a time sounded even better!*

We returned home hoping to be more relaxed, ready to start all over again. I worked with Nansie on a roster for Jack's medications, so I would do everything correctly, but by the end of it, I just lost the plot. We decided that it would be best to try again tomorrow, I felt like I was going around and around in circles.

It was so nice to have Jack home. We found that he wanted to stay in our bed with us, which was fine, because after being in the big hospital beds it seemed a bit odd and small to put him back into his cot. He slept with us, and although it was a little bit cramped, it was nice to have him close to me. It must have made him feel safe; it made me feel safe too. I told myself to rest and try not to think about what was to come and just be together. Just be together in this moment.

CHAPTER 10

Love is all there is. Every other emotion or feeling is a branch of love or a lack of love. Fear is the lowest and furthest emotion from love. When you choose your emotion towards an outcome, choose wisely, for all emotions are powerful. Will you choose love or fear to add to your life and its many complicated choices? Fear is the darkness and can only make things darker, while love is all-powerful, love is light, and love shines brightest in the dark.

Why did the time have to go so fast? I didn't ever want this week to begin, but Monday had arrived. Anthony's work had been good to us, and he had plenty of time to take off, so we could get a grip on this situation we were all in together. We fasted Jack from eight in the morning like we were told to do and went into the hospital to begin the GFR kidney function test.

When we arrived, the nurse explained that Jack would have numbing cream put on the tops of his hands and on the inside of the bends in his arms for about an hour. This was to help numb that area to put in an IV with less pain to Jack. They do lots of spots on kids just in case they can't find a vein. Then they would take blood from him every hour after that for the next three hours.

Then the nurse told us, "Make sure he eats and drinks plenty during the test."

"What?" I asked. "We have been instructed to fast him for a lumbar puncture test this afternoon! He hasn't eaten since eight o'clock this morning."

"Well, the whole test won't work if Jack doesn't have fluids in his body. He is supposed to eat and drink throughout the test, we must contact his doctor to discuss this."

Are you serious?

Far out. I tell you, I felt like the communication in this place was non-existent sometimes. The nurse returned and told us that Jack would have to have IV fluids for the whole period of the test. You know what that means, don't you? It means that instead of every hour just coming here and having some blood taken and then being able to leave and do as we please until the next hour, we had to stay there the whole time. For four bleeping hours!

Let me explain the room. It was the size of a cupboard, and it had a bucket of toys that were about twenty years old, which I was scared to even touch. We had to entertain Jack, a two-year-old who was frustrated just being still, unable to walk, and of course not allowed to eat and drink a single thing for four hours. Oh, this was going to be fun. We could have gone to the park or done different things if we were allowed to leave, but we couldn't. It was so frustrating!

We had allowed the numbing cream to sit for an hour, and even then, we practically had to hold Jack down on the bed while the doctor tried ever so hard to get an IV into the inside crease of his arm. Jack was screaming while they slowly poked the needle around and around, trying to find his vein. They failed miserably the first few times and then decided to start on the other arm. They finally found a vein and attached fluids into it. So, then it all began.

Do not ask me how we did it, but we did. It was a stressful and daunting experience. When we were walking in to have the last blood work taken from Jack for the test, I was relieved that it was soon going to be over. We had done whatever we could to play and sing and clap and read. Every toy had been used, and although he wanted food and his bottle, we were able to take his mind off of it and keep going. It was now 1:15 p.m. We had a physiotherapy booked in, so we raced up there so that Jack could do some fun games before going to have the lumbar puncture test at two o'clock.

We did a whole bunch of climbing and ball games with the physiotherapist, but after a small period of time, Jack was no longer up for it. He was hungry, and he wanted food or a bottle to make him happy. It was now nearly time for us to move on. We had almost succeeded in getting Jack to his appointment without food and drink and without a huge amount of screaming. I must admit he had been a true champion lasting the day. Anthony and I hadn't eaten either, because we couldn't eat in front of Jack. Being pregnant, I was completely starving.

It was almost two o'clock, and we decided to head over to the oncology area, which was an old heritage building situated outside next to the specialist hospital. We just got the pram through the slender doorway and were asked to sit down and wait. There were heaps of toys in this small room, which was helpful, and Jack could play once again with something different.

A different oncology doctor came and greeted us. She was the one who would be doing the lumbar puncture for us today. We followed her down a very narrow corridor, but at the end was this large room with four beds on the right and five big recliner chairs on the left. We then turned to the right and went into a small room with a bed and a desk. We all sat down, and we were ready. Oh, how we were ready to get this over and done with.

The doctor explained the test to us, and we were fine with it. They would give Jack this red syrup through a syringe, and it would make him drowsy, but he would still be awake.

"So how long have you had the cream on his back for?" the doctor asked.

Anthony and I just looked at each other, "Cream? What do you mean?"

"He has to have the white numbing cream on his back for at least an hour before we do the lumbar puncture."

Look out lady! My blood is boiling!

"I'm sorry," I said, "but no one has said anything to me about putting cream on his back!" I was *so* angry.

No one at any time had explained to us that this procedure would need the white numbing cream on his back. He was supposed to be under anaesthetic. I placed both my hands over my face and just smiled in disbelief. The doctor could see that I had now become completely ropeable.

"Jack hasn't eaten nor drunk anything since eight this morning, do you know how hard it was? We were told to fast him, and then we get to the GFR and they tell us that he has to eat. We have sat in a room for four hours with him attached to a drip, and now you are telling us that we have to go and come back in another hour?"

"I'm so sorry!" The doctor's apology was heartfelt. "I will get someone in here right now to put the cream on, and then you will have to return in an hour and we will do the lumbar puncture then."

I didn't understand. They were treating us like we knew what the hell we were doing, and we didn't, like we should be mind-readers or something. Why didn't they understand that we were just trying to survive this a moment at a time and that every moment counted? They just didn't understand how hard it had been today. No one did.

We watched as the nurses placed some of the cream on Jack's back. They were very precise about making sure it was on the right spot, so how the hell could we have ever done it and with what freaking cream? They covered it in a plastic tape to keep it there, which of course we also did not have, and off we went for a walk for another hour.

My emotions were red. I was steaming! I just wished they were organised so that all this added pressure was not put on our shoulders. Why couldn't they understand that? It was just too much to take, and now we had more stuff added from the people who were supposed to be helping us and guiding us through this. They were the professionals, weren't they?

We returned in an hour, and we were over it. We sat Jack on one of the beds in the big room at the end of the building hallway that I described earlier. We tried very slowly to get him to drink this red medication. Jack drank it well compared to what he would normally do. He was probably that hungry he would have taken anything, and so it didn't take long for the effects of the drug to kick in.

He was acting like he was drunk, holding up one hand in front of his face and saying, "Oooooooohhhh, wow, ten fingers!"

Although this may seem mean, we were having a good laugh over it. It was the first time for the whole day we just relaxed and had a giggle. We then took Jack into a side room just off of the big room called the examination room; it had a bed in it that we laid him down onto his side, so they could do the procedure to his back.

Anthony and I walked out after they had told us to leave and closed the door. We felt guilty and started to discuss how one of us should have stayed with him while it was happening. By the time I decided I should go back in, they were bringing Jack back out. I think it took around two minutes in whole. We were amazed, all the crap we had been through for the day, and the procedure took two whole minutes. Why did they have to forget to do it in the MRI in the first place? So much agony because somebody initially forgot. So frustrating!

Jack recovered slowly from the medication, and a lovely nurse came over and gave all three of us some biscuits to eat because we were all starving. Jack got stuck into them, and he enjoyed every little bit. He eventually got his bottle, and everybody was happy again.

While we waited for Jack to recover, we asked the nurse a couple of questions, and one of them was, "What does the port look like that Jack will have inserted under his skin to access the chemotherapy?"

"Oh, I have one here I think I can show you."

She went off and came back with a little case and opened it. She pulled out the port, and it was a great deal bigger than I thought it would be. The actual port was about the size of a twenty-cent piece, and it was around half a centimetre high. It had a small circular indent in the top like a cup where the chemotherapy would sit and then slowly run through a soft, slim catheter tube that goes through your vein; the catheter protects the large vein during the treatment.

I just can't believe that you have to go through so many traumas to continue the treatment. It just makes the fear in me explode. He could die just from having this stupid thing inserted.

Eventually after Jack slowly recovered from the anaesthetic we left the hospital, and it was almost five o'clock. It had been a massive day, but we had gotten through it, and we were all still in one piece and completely relieved to be going home.

The following day was great. The morning sessions of physiotherapy and speech therapy were cancelled and rescheduled for one in the afternoon. This meant we didn't have to spend the whole day at the hospital. We met up with our oncologist, Dr. Marlene, at two o'clock to discuss the lumbar puncture and the next day's proceedings. The lumbar puncture was all clear, and the GFR was normal. We discussed the process of the port, which was planned to be surgically inserted tomorrow. We would go to DOSA (day of surgery admission) in the morning.

Jack would need to fast from seven a.m. to go into surgery at one in the afternoon. Anthony and I had decided that I would stay with Jack overnight after the surgery, because Anthony had stayed so many times before. After this conversation with Dr. Marlene, we left, I had an appointment for my current pregnancy with my doctor at the private hospital we had chosen, all was going normally. We went home and waited for the day to come when Jack would once again have surgery.

CHAPTER 11

Your strong hands can lift up a weary body. Your soft words can ease a struggling mind. Your gentle hug can soothe a bleeding heart, and your gift of compassion can change a broken world. Never underestimate your worth. Everything that you do impacts the world and the people around you. You are an amazing piece of a great puzzle.

We arrived at DOSA the next morning around eleven o'clock as we had been asked to do and to my surprise, so did many other families. We went in and registered ourselves, and we were sent to a designated area in the room. The room had been split into four coloured sections. Two other families were waiting in our section.

We passed the time by playing in the little toy room, which was quite good, full of different things to do, loads of cars that Jack loved, and toys that were different from what Jack had at home. There was a little section with tables so that the children could do some craft work as well, which helped the time go quickly.

We were seen by the nurses to weigh Jack and measure his height, and then by the office people to do all the paperwork. Soon it was one o'clock. I was thinking how great it was that we had made it and that Jack would soon be going in to have his port procedure done. Jack must have been starving, again, and for him to not complain about not having his bottle had been a miracle. Every now and then he would ask for it, but we just changed the subject and took his mind away from it. We were getting good at that.

The time then started to pass very slowly. We saw an anaesthetist and asked what time Jack would go in, as we had been told that he would go in at one o'clock.

"You guys are third on the list today," he said.

"Third?" I questioned.

"There are two other operations before Jack's, so that means he should go in around three o'clock."

Oh shit! Here we go again!

I was shocked, I had just automatically thought that we were going to be called to go in at one o'clock. Were we supposed to just know that it would be later? We had never done this before, and now I felt like we weren't prepared.

"I don't understand why we had to fast Jack from seven this morning if he isn't having surgery until three?" I asked him.

"That's just the way they do it. It's just in case things change, the order of the operation may need to be changed, and if it does, everyone is prepared."

I was angry. I didn't know how this place worked. I just thought that you fast your child so that he would go in at the right time. If he was the third in, why not fast him from ten o'clock? Why wasn't I told he was the third one?

Jack started to get grumpy, who wouldn't? We weren't allowed to have any food and drink in there in front of all the children, which was completely understandable, we wouldn't want to go and eat anything before Jack did anyway. It didn't seem fair.

By around two o'clock, Jack had had just about enough of the waiting and not eating. Also, the child who was second on the list still had not gone in, so we knew we still had an hour wait at least. We asked the nurses if we could take Jack outside to the park to get some fresh air to take his mind off of eating. They told us that they were not allowed to let us leave the room in case we gave him something to eat or drink. I'm not an idiot, but apparently some people feel guilty and try to give their kids food and drink.

Anthony decided that he would fight this one. He promised that we would not give him anything, so they eventually agreed. We were able to waste time pushing Jack around the park creating a little bit of extra fun for the day. I snuck a sausage roll in for myself; while Anthony played with Jack. I crept away to the little deli at the front of the hospital. Anthony refused to eat until Jack ate, which was something that my dear little unborn child was not allowing me to do. I needed to eat, it had been far too long.

We returned to DOSA soon after and we were really happy about being able getting into the sunshine while wasting a little bit of time. Sad, isn't it, that we waste our time away and yet all we do is wish we had more of it?

We brought Jack back to DOSA and continued to play with him in the toy room. There we noticed another lady who had been waiting all day with her little boy. It got to the point where it was just them and us left out of all those people who had started here. We had a little chat about the horrible day we'd both had, and then she got called to go in. There was Anthony and I with Jack drawing on the craft tables looking at each other. We looked around the room as we sat, just the three of us and no one else.

The whole of DOSA looked like it had been evacuated, but there we were, still waiting. Even the volunteers had packed up and gone home for the day. The time hit 4:15 p.m. Yes, that's right, it was now 4:15 p.m. A time in my life that will be impossible for me to ever forget. My child, my little Jack, had not consumed an ounce of food or drink since seven that morning.

Finally, the nurse strolled up to us and said, "They are ready for Jack now."

Anthony and I did nothing but look at each other as we shifted our butts off those chairs and began walking down the corridor with Jack in Anthony's arms. These poor little children. The things we do to them are just terrible.

We were escorted to another room where, to our surprise, four of the other families were still waiting. There was the lady we had seen in the toy room and her little boy still waiting too. We filled out some more forms, and Anthony had to get dressed in a paper gown, cap, and shoes, as he would need to be there while Jack was put under the anaesthetic.

Amazingly, the doctors were ready for us and began to take Jack and Anthony through. The lady who was with her little boy went straight up to the nurse in charge and stated that she had been there a great deal longer than we had, but she did it in a very nice way.

"No offence," she said, and there was none taken.

I could understand completely. The funny thing was that we were the last in that DOSA room and yet the first to leave this one. The nurse explained that we were all assigned different groups of doctors and that Jack's had become available before everyone else's, even though they had been told to get prepared.

I smiled at the other mother and she smiled back, shrugging her shoulders. It appeared that this wonderful system had been a bit sluggish today, it is to be expected at times, but it was so very frustrating. Now for once it felt like we weren't always the last ones in the room.

Anthony returned, and as we went to leave, we wished the woman well. It was time for food, and we set straight up towards the café to fill our famished bodies. On our way back after about a half hour, we went for a little stroll around the corridors to buy some time until Jack would return to the hospital's recovery section. You would not believe it, but there we passed that lady and her little boy from DOSA once again. My mouth hit the floor. She made eye contact with us and stopped. I looked down, as her son was eating his little heart out.

"That was quick!" I said to her.

She shook her head at us and replied, "No, he never went in. It ended up being cancelled due to them not being able to get another doctor or something."

"Are you serious? After all that time? I can't believe it!"

"I have to come back another day, so we are going home!"

She smiled, and we let her go. That poor woman, after such a long day and her little boy not being able to eat anything, it was cancelled! I even felt a little bit guilty. Of course, it wasn't my fault, but wow, how bad was that?

We waited in the hallway just out the front of where Jack would be brought through the recovery doors. They soon opened, and you could hear Jack from a mile away. He was not a fan of seeing strange people dressed in blue suits, wondering where on earth his mummy and daddy had disappeared to.

We both ran quickly towards him as we heard the nurses saying to him, "Look, Jack, who's that? It's Mummy and Daddy!"

He was up on his knees on the bed crying while they wheeled him down the corridor. I quickly ran to him and held his hand until we got into the unit that was like a second recovery area. I picked him up and held him to me. He enjoyed his milk, which unfortunately came straight back up again.

When Jack had recovered a little more within the recovery unit, we were transferred across the hallway to a four-shared room within the recovery ward. This ward was quite new, and although we were sharing this room with three other people, it had a huge sense of peacefulness about it. It was nothing like the other wards we had experienced not too long ago.

I had chosen to stay with Jack that night, and I was nervous because I had not done so by myself since this had all happened. He was still being a bit sicky, and to the disapproval of the nurses, we would still give him watered-down milk. We gave him whatever he wanted. This child had been starved, but he would still vomit mildly. It wasn't too bad, really. He had eaten a small amount when he first initially came to the recovery ward, some custard and a small amount of a vegemite sandwich, but not a great deal. He just loved his bottle of milk!

It was time for everyone to go home for the night, and I lay down on the bed with Jack, even though the rules stated that we really shouldn't be doing that.

So frickin' what! I'll do as I please for my kid to be happy and comfortable.

He loved us lying with him. Jack felt more comfortable and safe in this horrible place with me by his side cuddling him. It was definitely uncomfortable at times, but I guarantee you that it was a whole lot better than those fold-out beds they had going on here.

During the night, Jack had another watered-down bottle that he held down, and he continued to sleep quite well. He wasn't disrupted by me moving and fidgeting all the time. Being pregnant did not help the comfort factor in this situation.

In the early hours of the morning, Jack ended up lying on his back. I noticed that I had fallen asleep for a period of a couple of hours and that Jack had remained on his back for the whole time. He awoke, and when he did, I saw the back of his head where his incision was had changed. I felt it slowly and noticed that all the gooey fluid was gone, it was normal again. I couldn't believe it; the pressure from sleeping on his back had forced all the fluid to drain away. Getting a shunt for the fluids would no longer be an issue, how wonderful.

It had been a good night, I must say, with Jack sleeping very well. The room, although with its occasional noises, was very peaceful. I don't understand how one ward could be so different from another. It was still a shared room with three other people, but the atmosphere was so pleasant to me. It really made such a difference to how you were mentally and physically the next day.

I did not get a fantastic sleep, but I felt great in the overall of things, Jack too. Anthony had come in early, and I was able to have a quick shower there before we started all the arrangements to check out and go home. When we were leaving, we went into the lift just as Ian was, and so we showed him the back of Jack's head. He was impressed and very happy that the fluid was gone.

"There was another little girl who was diagnosed with the same tumour as Jack today," he said.

"Another one?" Anthony asked. "A medulloblastoma?"

"Yes!" Ian said.

"How old is she?" I asked.

"She is seven."

"Isn't it strange that a tumour so rare has been found twice within such a small period of time?"

"They are rare, but they are tumours that affect children," he said. "But when they come is when they come." We spoke briefly about Jack overall, and then we each went on our way.

We went home knowing that we would be back again the very next day for another appointment for speech therapy and physiotherapy. There was also the need to take an X-ray of Jack's chest to ensure that the port had been placed in the correct position. The port was such an odd thing. It protruded out of Jack's skin quite largely, and I wondered how he could ever possibly sleep or lay on it without it hurting him. It must have been why he slept on his back for so long last night. I guess he would just get used to it being there.

The next day went smoothly with the X-ray. Anthony had to put a vest on just like Jack did, while I stood in the booth with the guy who was operating it. I did not feel comfortable being anywhere near the X-ray machine being pregnant, but the operator assured me that where I was would be safe. The X-ray showed that the port's position was good. We were home by early afternoon, which was very nice; we could have a little bit of time all to ourselves, although it was a tiny bit scary knowing that tomorrow would be Jack's very first day of chemotherapy.

We also needed to have a hearing test beforehand and a physiotherapy appointment. We really weren't too sure of what to expect with the chemotherapy. We had spoken about things with Dr. Marlene, but you really don't know how it will all go. Anthony's mum was a little wary of

Jack having the chemotherapy and the radiotherapy; she thought I should do some investigating into a more natural approach to healing Jack. The thing is, I didn't know anything. It sounded terrible what we were expected to go through at the hospital, but we were in the hands of the professionals, and this was the way they were telling us to go. If I chose not to do that, then I as a mother would not have done everything possible to save my child.

CHAPTER 12

Being complacent keeps us comfortable and safe. It's nice to feel warm and cosy in life, unfortunately our souls want to grow and experience. The only way to do this is to step out of our comfort zone into the unknown where we can experience the world in all of its glory.

Anthony was always searching on the Internet about the same tumour that Jack had. He looked up people who had survived and others who didn't, statistics on the survival rate, and pictures of the anatomy of it. The statistics for Jack were around 65 to 85 per cent survival rate. Out of all the stories he read, there was only one who had been in remission, and a few others going through the treatment. The others had passed away.

Anthony told me there was a story of a couple in another country whose child needed to undergo chemotherapy. He was two years of age, and with the same brain tumour as Jack. The couple both had a medical background or were in medical professions, and they chose not to give the chemotherapy to their child. Instead, they put him through a natural cancer treatment that was available to them. The problem was that the government was taking legal action to force them to stop the natural treatment and start chemotherapy. If they did not, they would be accused of child neglect.

I remembered what was said to me in the hospital by the lady doctor in emergency: "If we don't find anything at all wrong with Jack, he won't be coming home with you."

Realising that you may not be in control is very scary. How can you decide what is best for your child when everyone else has already decided for you, whether you like it or not?

Anthony's idea of studying the tumour and all the stories and statistics were just making things worse for me. I cried for ages. There was nothing positive at all, and I couldn't help Jack without believing that he would be just fine. I chose to do all I could and do one thing at a time, step by step. Let's get this treatment done as well as we could and just do what we had to do to survive a day at a time.

Jack's hearing test was in the same area where we went within the hospital to get his eyes checked, it was packed. I was a bit worried that if they ran the same way, we would be here for hours, and with so much being on today, I just didn't have the time. We sat in the waiting room after telling the lady at the desk that we had arrived, and as I was placing my bottom onto the chair I heard, "Jack please."

Woohoo are you serious? I thought to myself.

I stared up at the lady who had called out Jack's name waiting to make sure she had gotten it right. With a small smile on my face, I grabbed our things and went in. There were a few unpleasant faces staring at us from the waiting room.

"I can't believe how quick it was! Usually when we come to this section for Jack's eyes, we are waiting here for hours!"

The lady smiled. "Oh yes, it's different for us, it doesn't take too long."

Right at this moment she was my favourite person in the world. She took us into a soundproof room and did all kinds of funny things to get Jack to cooperate, but sometimes a two-year-old is in charge. Jack did very well to start off with, but he lost interest. The lady was happy with the outcome and told us that she had tested many two-year-old's before who were all very much the same. Anthony and I were so happy that it had gone so well. Jack had great hearing, and we were leaving the area to walk around a little before the physiotherapy appointment started at ten thirty. There was still the nagging feeling of having to start Jack on chemotherapy.

Why, God, couldn't you have just given us a break? Why did you allow Jack to have to go through this?

Sadly, it seemed that we were really going to have to do the whole hog. I could not believe that Jack would lose his hair; he was going to be one of those kids who keeps a small amount and still looks good.

Isn't he? Isn't he, God?

After all our appointments, we made our way down to the small heritage building that we had been to before for Jack's lumbar puncture. This was where Jack would have all of his chemotherapy. Wow, it was a great deal busier than it had been the last time we had come. There were so many kids here, and they were all different. Some had hair and there were some with none, some with tubes down their noses, some in wheelchairs, and some who appeared to be so sick that they looked like they were ninety years old. I did not like it here.

Although there were toys everywhere and Jack enjoyed playing, it was hard to know where to look and how to think. The fear would just surround you. How do you not cry until you can no longer cry anymore after seeing such suffering in so many little faces? The room was small; I couldn't understand why such an important section of medicine for so many kids had been cramped into a tiny building. I went to the front desk to let them know we were there, and we sat down to wait our turn.

When it was time to go in, Dr. Marlene called for us, and we went up the very narrow hallway, around a corner, and through the rabbit warren. I didn't realise that we would wait for so long. It must have been a busy day. We went through Jack's schedule quickly with Dr. Marlene, and then it was into the large chemotherapy administration room at the end for Jack's first dose of chemotherapy. His port had to be accessed, and there had been no numbing cream put onto it, so that Jack would not feel the needle going in. Once again, we had not been told what to do or even been given the cream.

They gave Jack the red oral medication that would sedate him to a point where he wouldn't feel it. It was so hard and time-consuming to get him to slowly take the medication, but it worked. Then for the first time they accessed the port that had been recently surgically placed under his skin.

We had to go through to the examination room, which joined off from the main big chemotherapy administering room. This examination room is where they did all the accessing and de-accessing of the ports; it was where Jack had had his lumbar puncture done previously. Jack lay on the bed, and the nurses had a tray of things they were going to use for the accessing of this port. First it was a needle that was about two centimetres long and bent at a 90-degree angle. It was attached to a clear plastic-looking butterfly. The butterfly had a thin long tube about seven centimetres long that had a little knob on the end that you could attach to fluids or put medication through.

When they stuck the needle through his skin and into the port, I was just so glad that Jack would not remember much about it, because as I held his hand it looked like it hurt. They put a folded-up swab underneath the butterfly because there was a small distance between his skin where the needle went in to where the plastic butterfly sat. It was like a little cushion for it. Then they used long sticky strips to hold it in place, and then they covered it with a big rectangular plastic sticker.

The long tube hung out so that the nurses could access it easily. They all called it a tail. In my mind, I could not understand how all of this could not have been made simpler. There was so much to do before you even began the treatment. I thought of the human race as a wonderful species that was always coming up with medical breakthroughs. Sadly, at this particular moment, I was thinking that we had made things way too complicated.

I'm no doctor, and I know little about medicine, but I felt let down. It was probably because of my lack of knowledge about it all, but why weren't we smarter? Jack needed to have two hours of fluids before we even started the chemotherapy, and it hit four o'clock before the first chemotherapy drug was pumped into his tiny body. We had arrived at this building around eleven thirty in the morning. There had been a great deal of waiting, again.

There were a few different drugs that Jack would need to have: vincristine, cisplatin, cyclophosphamide, and etoposide. The first one, which was vincristine, would have to be readministered seven days after today and then seven days after that day and then a week's rest. The great thing was that after fluids, it only took fifteen minutes to administer. It was the only drug within this chemotherapy cycle that would be repeated after today within the clinic. Etoposide would have to be administered every day after day two for three weeks through Jack's nasal gastric tube, which we would do ourselves at home at night time before bed.

This initial cycle of chemotherapy within the hospital would ultimately take around thirty-nine hours, because it would include many hours of hydration. Vincristine had many short-term side effects, like bone and abdominal pain, fever, and mouth sores. After the vincristine had been given, the next chemotherapy drug was cisplatin. This was the drug that could cause some permanent side effects like high-pitched hearing loss or, worse, fertility and kidney problems.

The third chemotherapy drug would be cyclophosphamide, followed by etoposide. Both could cause infertility but also had many of the same short-term side effects as the others, like hair loss, low blood counts, and pain.

This was all very scary to me. Jack had already been through so much, and now instead of just worrying ourselves with his brain tumour, we had to worry about all the side effects of his medicine as well. Am I the only one who finds this weird? Shouldn't the medicine we depend on help us? In our normal little lives, we get a cold, so we take things to help. When we hurt ourselves, we fix it. Simple, isn't it? No, not anymore. Life had become so complicated.

I think that I was just as afraid of Jack's medicine as I was of his tumour. I should not feel this way! I should feel relieved that I was starting his cure, but would this be his cure or his killer?

We had been in the clinic all day. It was now five in the evening. Once again, we were the last to remain. With the nurse assisting us, we took Jack up to the chemotherapy ward that he would call home for the next two nights. Anthony carried him while the nurse wheeled his drip and his monitor alongside him. We made our way through the small corridor and outside. We walked towards the doors to the hospital, through them and then up the elevators to level two, where we walked down a long hallway past the cafeteria and finally down to the chemotherapy ward. We had been told that this ward was a great deal better than the other wards we had encountered within this hospital and that it was quite new.

At first sight, it was very peaceful. It had a nurse's station and a corridor with individual room doors. We were put into our first room here, and I must admit it was like a hotel room compared to all the others we had experienced. This one was a single room with a TV, a bed, a big single fold-out recliner chair, and a private bathroom with toilet and shower. Wow, I could not believe it! It was Fantastic!

We entertained Jack with balloons flying around the room. He also had a few visitors that night, which was a great distraction. He was doing well with his food and his fluids, and his temperature stayed normal.

We were told that the next day we would need to start a mouth-care regimen with Jack. During these times we could not be able to clean Jack's teeth properly with a brush because of the low blood counts that could cause problems if you cut your gums. The blood is unable to clot as well as it normally does if your platelets become very low. There was mouthwash and gel to use, with huge cotton buds to apply it with. I wasn't sure how Jack would cope with that, but we would start trying tomorrow. Painful mouth ulcers could come about without it, and I really wanted to do the right thing for Jack.

His nappy had to be changed at least every three to four hours because of the liquids going through him. The nurses had to make sure that he was urinating regularly, another side effect of chemotherapy was difficulties with urinating. How was Anthony going to change Jack throughout the night without him waking up? It was going to be a challenge, and as we told the nurses, Jack would never let anyone he didn't know do it.

I was told that because I was pregnant, I shouldn't be doing nappy changes and administering drugs; there would be chemotherapy within his urine, poop, and vomit.

How can I not to do these things for Jack? I thought. *I won't have people with me every second of the day.*

I was instructed to be very cautious and make sure that if I did at any stage have to change him, I wore gloves and washed my hands thoroughly afterwards.

The cisplatin was still going. Soon, Jack would start his cyclophosphamide, and tomorrow his etoposide. I left Anthony and went home, returning the next day with Nansie so that she could help me with all the things that I was not really supposed to do. Jack had slept well from eight last night until six this morning. I had brought in some things for Jack to do, even though there was a toy room within the ward that you could take toys from to play with.

It started out to be an average kind of day, but soon it became a hard, long one. Nansie and I were really prepared and documented everything on the whiteboard, just like Anthony had done the night before. This was so we wouldn't forget to do anything or forget what had happened during the day and at what time. Jack vomited three times that morning. We were trying to get used to his reactions, so we could anticipate his vomiting. We didn't want a bed and clothing change every single time, but that is what was happening.

We would change his nappy every four hours, but changed that to every three, as his nappy would leak, and he would need another change of clothing. I rang Anthony to bring in more clothes for him. There was also a laundry where we could wash all his clothes if we needed to down the hall, praise the lord! I did not realise that there would be so many accidents. Nansie was kept very busy, and I did a lot of stuff to help, which she continued to tell me off for.

Jack spent most of his time either sitting on us or us sitting in bed with him. He loved to be close to us, and even though my ankles were becoming cankles, it was nice to have him close. That afternoon, Jack had to have a nasal gastric tube put down his nasal passage, which went all the way down to his stomach. That night he would need to have his etoposide medication administered through it.

They took Jack to a room that had a bed in it and where they had painted all the walls with brightly coloured fish and sea animals. It was really nice. The nurses went ahead with the nasal gastric tube while Nansie and I watched and held on to Jack tightly. It was one of the most horrific things you could ever watch your kid go through! My poor little Jack, as if he hadn't been through enough, he now had to have a tube pushed down his throat while they tried to make him drink through a syringe to help with the whole gagging reaction.

He started gagging repeatedly, and all I could imagine was him doing one huge massive vomit everywhere! He had already been vomiting all day due to the chemotherapy. After a few attempts, it was over. The nurses taped the tube down along his cheek and tucked it around his ear and pinned it to his clothes. I looked at him in awe. How was this kid supposed to stay like this? For the whole of his treatment with this thing down his throat? They just couldn't be serious about this! I would have been gagging non-stop.

Nansie and I took Jack back to his room, where I just lay with him on the bed. He had not eaten much all day, and every time he did, he would vomit. I did not want him to vomit anymore with this stupid tube down his throat. It must have been irritating him and making him feel like he wanted to throw up. What happened if he just vomited the tube up? Well, back down they would shove it!

The day was not ending well. With Jack's temperature deciding to go up to 39.4 degrees, the nurses had started giving him two regular drugs alternatively: ondansetron and Maxolon for nausea. He was started on paracetamol, which the nurses put through his nasal gastric tube, resulting in Jack vomiting it straight back up. They repeated it through his IV line within his port instead, which worked well. It was now time for his etoposide.

Shit, this should be fun!

They administered it through the nasal gastric tube into his stomach, with fluids before and after to make sure that no drug was left in the tube. It took a whole twenty minutes before Jack hurled that up also.

Here's the thing: if you vomit before twenty minutes, you can readminister the drug, but if it is after that, you have to assume that the body has done somewhat of a job to take it in. So, Jack was left alone without readministering the etoposide drug, which I am glad about ... I think! So, let's have some thoughts on this? Anyone? OK, well, here is mine:

This kid is not allowing anything to stay down. He must be starving and in a great deal of pain, and yet we just keep at him with more and more things! They have a drug that needs to go down but can't stay down because the side effect of all the other drugs in his chemotherapy cycle is vomiting! So, they put down a tube into his guts, which can be vomited up quite easily, to administer the chemotherapy drug etoposide through it, as kids won't take it orally, and this drug causes vomiting also. We then give more drugs to stop the vomiting, which really doesn't seem to be stopping the vomiting at all! What side effects do they have?

And now, even though I hate him having all these stupid drugs, he takes etoposide and vomits it up within twenty minutes, which means he may not have even got that drug into his system! Does that mean he's not getting the stuff that is supposed to stop his brain tumour from coming back? Is it going to grow back if we don't readminister it? What the hell!

I thought I was stupid, but this was the most stupid thing I had ever seen in my entire life. I was so confused! At least now you all know what goes on in the minds of all us parents who don't understand. I didn't want the etoposide readministered, and yet I did.

Nansie and I left quite late, and so I decided to stay at her house. It was just too much to take, and to be alone in a cold house would have made it worse. I know that this seems bad, but there was a small four-letter word that I felt like screaming out to this wonderful God of ours, with of course a complementary middle-finger gesture.

What on earth are you doing up there, big man? What are you trying to do to us? The human race is pathetic, I get it, I understand. How rude of me to think that we could possibly come up with some sort of uncomplicated version of medication for cancer. We suck! And guess what, big man—you created us! Ha!

Oopsy, there's that rare form of anger again. That social worker was right. Man, she is good!

CHAPTER 13

Days feel longer than others, yet years fly by so fast. In the time that you have left know that you are blessed to be breathing and even more blessed if you are given the gift of growing old. It is never too late to do all of the wonderful things that you have wanted to do. Now is the time to do them.

When the morning came, after a hot shower, it was just natural for me to start all over again. How could this be? Was it because I tried not to think too deeply into it? Wouldn't my natural reaction be to fall in a heap and refuse to cope with it all? No, not for a mother who needs to see her baby well again. I would do anything for Jack, anything to save him from this horrible disease that no one could tell me how he got in the first place. There were never any answers, and that was one of the hardest things to deal with.

Why?

Because there was no one to blame and nothing to stop so that it wouldn't have ever happened or happen again. If I knew why this happened, then I could change what caused it. I could make it better.

Jack continued to be lethargic all day and didn't do much more than lie around and watch different kids movies on the TV. His temperature skyrocketed to 40.1 degrees, and the doctors and nurses all thought he had some kind of virus as well as having to deal with the chemotherapy. Normally we would be going home today, but there was no way Jack would be going anywhere with a temperature that high.

He was then considered infectious. We were isolated within his room, unable to use any of the facilities within the rest of the ward. The doctors and nurses all wore gowns and masks whenever they came in to see him. It's funny how the time ticks by and all you're doing is just looking forward to each moment of the day. Like a cup of tea at ten in the morning and then lunch delivered at noon and then another cup of tea at three. We really couldn't do much at all, we just had to come up with creative things we could do while Jack was in bed.

The moveable food-tray table that went around the bed was great. We could leave Jack in bed while he drove his cars along it and then let them crash off the edge down onto the bed near his side. He appeared better, but whenever he tried to eat and drink, he would have an occasional vomit, even though he was tolerating small amounts.

The day was long and hard, especially when it became night time for Nansie and I to go home. Jack didn't want us to go, after we had been with him all day. I know that Anthony found it hard being alone with Jack, trying to occupy him until he went to sleep. It was difficult to help Jack understand that he couldn't leave the room because he was connected to his pump, this restricted how far he could go within the room. Ma and Pa would come in on some nights to help out with blowing balloons and letting them go, which made it easier for Nansie and I to sneak out.

The next morning, we saw that Anthony had done a whole heap of drawings on the big board on the wall for Jack. Nansie and I continued to entertain Jack like that throughout the day. We decided to bring in his chair again, the one that sat on the dining chair at home, and we attached it to one of the chairs in the room. Jack had a great time being able to sit up and do things on the table. We also brought in sticker books, which he loved to do.

The windowsill was thick enough to drive cars along it and make them crash and fall onto the ground. Jack could stand up and hold onto it for balance. We came up with so many different ideas to get him through the day.

Today, Jack had to have a test done up his nose, which was to see if he had any viruses. I had never experienced this one before and really didn't know what to expect. First, the lady did a finger-prick test for blood, because the nurses had found it extremely hard to draw blood from Jack's butterfly in his port. The lady then had to stick this thing up Jack's nose for the test. It was terrible.

"You might want to hold him while I do this, because it's not very comfortable," she had said.

Jack was sitting in his chair, so I held his hands while Nansie jumped around the room making noises to distract him. This device was like a vacuum with its loud sucking noise, and Jack just screamed and cried while she quickly stuck it up one of his nostrils. His nose had a small bleed, and I put my arm around him.

"My poor baby! It's okay," I said.

We wiped his nose, and before too long he was ready to eat again. Thank goodness he recovered quickly. He had a small amount of soup and began to want half a vegemite sandwich, so I gave it to him. He ate it with no concern. I loved to watch him eat, because I had never seen him eat that well before. I was so proud of him, even though after a few hours we saw it all again as he had a vomit. I was happy that he had kept it down for a little while.

The doctors came and advised us that there had not been any indication of a virus in his bloods, that's why they requested the nose test. They would have to wait for the results. They also explained to me that we would have to administer all Jack's medications at home. Before we left the hospital, we would have a doctor coming in to explain each drug carefully to us. They had a good feeling that Jack might be able to go home sometime tomorrow, his temperature had settled down.

The next day, Jack had another finger-prick blood test. We then had fun with Jamie, who did his physiotherapy treatment in his room with him. All day we were anxious to be let free from this prison. The nurses informed us that we would be going home today, it was now Tuesday, two days longer than what was planned. I let Anthony know that he wouldn't have to come back in for a night stay. What a relief! I made sure I had packed everything up neatly and put it all together, so we could just grab everything and go when we needed to.

Late that afternoon, I was given a huge pack of drugs that Jack had to have. There were also all the syringes of etoposide that were individually sealed and then sealed again in a dark black bag. We had waited all day for the all-clear to go home. We thought that it wasn't ever going to happen, and as it drew later we were thinking that we were going to have to stay another night.

After a whole lot of running around, we finally had everything we needed, which included ondansetron and Maxolon for vomiting; paracetamol; Bactrim; eye drops; lactulose for constipation; a box of water canisters and syringes to flush Jack's nasal gastric tube; blue strips of paper to test stomach fluids each time before and after the etoposide; mouth care, which consisted of a thick gel and a mouthwash with large mouth swabs and small cups; tape for the nasal gastric tube in case we needed to readjust it; a tube of the white numbing cream and patches for the next time we had to access his port; and not to forget, of course, those etoposide syringes and a yellow drug bin to throw the syringes out after we had used them.

Phew!

A doctor came in and explained it all to Nansie and I. The amounts were all stuck easily to read on the sides of each medication. The nurses had been quite good throughout our stay with showing us and allowing us to do most things that we would need to do for Jack. The doctor reconfirmed how to test stomach fluids and flush and administer through the gastric tube as well. There was so much medication that I became concerned about being robbed on the way out.

We sat and waited for a nurse to come in and take out Jack's butterfly connection to his port. It felt like forever, the time hit four o'clock and we were finally given the all-clear to go home.

Why did everything take so long!

It was wonderful being home, so different, just like freedom. Even though we would have to return the next day for another finger-prick blood test and a physiotherapy appointment, it was always better knowing that we could go home at the end of the day.

But wait! As it turned out, we did not have to return to the hospital the next day, after Jamie cancelled our physio appointment. I spoke with Dr. Marlene and she told us not to worry about the finger prick test either. We spent the day around the house. Jack had been eating well, with no real repercussions. When it got to dinnertime he was asking for a small kid's yoghurt, which he had always loved to have.

As I was handing it to Jack Anthony said, "Don't give him that!"

"Why not?" I asked.

"His stomach will still be funny from the chemotherapy and that will probably make it worse!"

Trying to take it from Jack now was a nightmare. He screamed in anger, and so I just let him have it. Two seconds later he vomited it all back up...including the nasal gastric tube!

Oh shit!

I couldn't believe it. Pulling the rest of that tube out was just terrible. It was half in and half out, terrible!

"You can go back into the hospital now, I'm not!" Anthony declared.

He definitely was not happy with me. I didn't think it was quite necessary to rub it in like that, but he was hard and refused to go with me to the hospital to have Jack's nasal gastric tube put back in. Luckily, Nansie was there, and she drove Jack and I back in, all the way to the hospital after I had called to let them know that we would be coming in.

And I thought today was the one day we wouldn't have to go to the hospital!

We had to go through the emergency department, and we had to make sure that Jack was put into a room by himself with us while we waited. This was because of his low blood levels and the fact that the doctors were still unsure if he had a virus. He had to be isolated from any infectious people and the emergency department was full of them. The gastric tube needed to be put back in, because he still needed to have his etoposide put through tonight after he fell asleep.

It didn't take long before we were seen, and a nurse who really didn't show much emotion or personality just shoved the tube down Jack's throat. It was shocking. Jack was screaming and choking and gagging on this stupid thing. Nansie was in tears, unable to watch him as she turned away and could no longer help me hold him down. It finally went down. I said to myself that I never wanted to see Jack go through that again. We drove home and arrived just after seven o'clock. Jack fell asleep on Anthony, and even though I shouldn't have, I administered his etoposide to him through his tube and we put him to bed.

I was always worried whenever I changed Jack's nappy, cleaned up his vomit, or gave him his etoposide. It was insane to think that I could never do these things. I know that I was pregnant and always thought about the repercussions of being so involved with and exposed to such powerful drugs. During this time all I could think about was what had to be done at the time. I was careful and did everything the way I was told to do so that I would be protected. I knew by the way Nansie and Anthony acted that they too did not want to administer the etoposide to Jack. It scared me also, but it had to be done, and so I did it.

After such a long night, we had to return the next day once again to the hospital for an eye appointment. Great! There went half the day! My appointment was for 9:50 in the morning, but we saw the first doctor at 10:15 and then the actual doctor we were supposed to see at about 10:45. She decided that she wanted to put drops in Jack's eyes, which meant we had to go away for an hour and then come back and wait to see her again. Then she checked both of his eyes, with the final outcome being to continue to patch his eye every day for two hours.

Really? The whole day wasted to tell me to keep doing what I was already doing.

We tried so hard to patch his eye and keep it on for as long as we could by using all kinds of bribes, but some days were unbearable. Jack would just rip it off. There would be days where Jack would tear at my skin to stop me from putting the patch on, and the moment just ended up with me bleeding and being completely stressed out. It was good, that the only thing to accomplish today was the eye appointment. We went home to get ourselves ready for the next day, which would be Friday again. This meant we would have to come into the hospital for Jack's vincristine chemotherapy. Onward we go!

CHAPTER 14

Patience...all will be revealed to you in time. It takes time to learn. It takes time to master. It takes time to grow. It takes time to understand what it is that you truly need and want from your life. Everything blooms in its own given time, even you. Be patient.

I was surprised that our day took so long, with only having blood work and vincristine treatment. This was taking around four or five hours for us, even though his treatment only really took about forty-five minutes to complete. Jack had to have blood taken first then we would wait an hour for the results. This was to show that he was healthy enough to have the Vincristine. In total it added up to about an hour and forty-five minutes maximum that we should have been at the hospital for, but there was always the waiting.

It always seemed like there were too many kids for such a small little waiting room. Waiting, waiting, waiting in the waiting room. Whoever came up with the name of the waiting room didn't really have to think much about it, because it was so obvious. Patients, well, I guess they knew you would have to have a great deal of *patience* to be a patient in the waiting room. My patience was running out.

The idea was to somehow get myself into a system: a system of waiting for long periods of time at different venues of the hospital. I had to come up with ideas to make sure that Jack got through each different stage. First, you go up to have blood taken. Jack would have a finger-prick done; it was quick and easy there and not much waiting around. Jack loved all the different posters on the walls of the rooms and things hanging from the ceiling, which was a great distraction. Then we would go to the toilets on the same level and change his nappy, and then put the white numbing cream on his port. The cream would take an hour to work, and it would take an hour for the blood results to come through again.

It would then be coffee-break time at the hospital café until the whole hour was up and then down to the oncology department, right on time for our appointment. Who was I kidding? They were never seeing me on time! Jack would play with the toys as we slowly watched the time tick by.

What is the point of giving me an appointment when we were never seen anywhere near that time?

Eventually we would be seen by Dr. Marlene or an acting oncologist. Jack would get a quick check over, and we would discuss Jack's blood work. The levels had to be good; he would not have treatment if the blood counts were too low.

All his levels were good today, and Jack would have his second dose of vincristine. We went into the room where they administered the chemotherapy, and we tried to get a bed for Jack, because he still needed a nap during the day. Getting him to sleep in a bed was so much easier than in one of the big recliners.

We watched the time tick by once again, and then Jack got his port accessed, and then we waited. Then he had his treatment, and then we waited. Then it would finish, and they would disconnect him, and then we would wait and wait and wait for him to have his butterfly removed. Then we would leave, finally being able to go home.

The weekend was great at home, just mucking about and not having to be anywhere. We could do what we wanted. Jack's hair had shown no signs of falling out yet, and I was so happy about that. We continued his etoposide every night but found it hard when one of us had to go out for the evening. We tried to make sure that we were both home when it had to be done, because it was a hard job to do. We tried to make it a routine to give it to Jack when he was asleep, because otherwise he would just vomit it up.

By Sunday night, Jack had become a little unsettled, and his temperature was starting to rise. We dosed him up with paracetamol and let him lay in our bed because he was distressed. By about two in the morning, his temperature had risen over the acceptable level to 39.5 degrees. I called the chemotherapy ward to let them know. The plan was to wait for another dose of paracetamol and redo his temperature, so I did. It was still too high.

We were told to bring him into the emergency department, and they would ring forward to warn of our arrival. We went straight through to a bay because there was no one at all in the emergency department waiting. We were taken into a room where Jack lay on the bed and tried to sleep while we once again waited. After many hours, early into that morning, after answering all the questions of the emergency doctors, we were taken up to the chemotherapy ward. We were put into a contained room where we were not allowed to use the ward's facilities, and the doctors and nurses wore gowns in case Jack had a virus.

The days had become very long. They slowly ticked by, and we felt like prisoners. We found out that Jack did have a virus, and he was started on an antibiotic for it. He continued to be low, with outbursts of happiness and lots of rest. The room we were given was great, with the white writing board closer to the ground so that it was easily reached by Jack. We pulled the trolley along that he was attached to and placed a rug on the ground where he could sit or stand and draw all over the whiteboard.

We played every game we could think of to keep him busy, and just for me to say, I was quite impressed with Jack. Although he was a two-year-old and had his moments that seemed unbearable, he was quite a patient little boy. What other kid would play alone in a tiny little room day after day? I was proud of him.

Days passed by, and slowly the virus began to set in with Anthony, and then with me. We were all very ill. Anthony got over it well, but I seemed to just be holding onto it. I had gotten so sick and was glad that Nansie was with me during the days, so I could sleep next to Jack while he slept. I continued to go back to Nansie's house each night to rest and then returned in the morning.

On Thursday, I noticed that Jack's hair had started to come out in my fingers, only mildly though. I thought that it might just become quite thin but still stay nice enough for him to look like himself. Jack's blood work had become bad, and the doctors were discussing a blood transfusion.

Oh man! Please no!

It's something I really didn't want Jack to have, but he'd already had one during his operation. Did it really matter? If he needed to have one, then he needed to have one.

It worried me what Ma would think, even though when she was told about the possible blood transfusion she appeared quite calm about it. Was she just putting on a brave face? My whole life, and I know you know what I'm talking about, you try to please everyone. I did not want to cause any disruption, especially with us going through such a hard time. We always got on so well individually and as a family. There was one problem, though: no matter how long or how much Ma spoke to me about God and her religion, I knew that she could never, ever make me change the way I believed.

I actually enjoyed our interesting chats about what we each believed, and it never bothered me. It's like I had created my own love for God through my own experiences and how my life was. Although at the moment, I was a little upset with him!

Nansie is a huge Catholic believer. She used to go to church every day, and she always believed in the rules of the church. I think she was scared into it. Back in the day you believed that God would punish you if you didn't fast before church or go to church every Sunday. Even though I grew up with Nansie's Catholic fears I just don't believe all that. Ma believes in many different things as a Jehovah Witness, her beliefs that she discusses with me I also don't believe in.

Why should God have to choose between so many great and wonderful people to save? They are all his children, aren't they? So, if I promoted God by being good and true and living by his rules, why should I not be standing by his side after I die? And I will.

I want to tell you a story, a moment in my youth that I remember like it was yesterday...

I was lying on my side on my brother's bed in his room, and my mother was kneeling in front of the bed facing me. She was reading me a story. Suddenly, I began to scream. I turned and stuffed my head into my hands in the pillow.

"What on earth is wrong?" she asked as she tried to pull me to face her.

"I don't want to look at you!" I screamed.

My mother was obviously concerned by my sudden reaction, but I knew why I was afraid to look at her.

"Don't be silly!" she said. "Now what's wrong with you?"

I slowly peered out of my hands, afraid to look at her, but it was gone. I told her that I had seen a golden light that went from one side of her neck around her head and ended by touching the other side of her neck. I was afraid, as it was so clear and so bright. My mother was full of peace.

"You saw a halo around my head!" she said.

"No, that's not a halo. A halo is above your head."

"No!" she said. "I will show you."

She ran and grabbed a couple of holy pictures of different saints, and sure enough, those saints' halos were glowing from neck to neck and not like a circle above your head. I felt calm now, and I realised that it must have been a good thing because my mother was so happy. I wasn't even six years old at the time.

For me, there was no need to explain God or the existence of a greater being, I already knew he was there. He had shown me. I made my judgments on my own and through my own experiences.

I believe that no one should ever say to someone else, "That's wrong or that is not true!" How could they really know? Through the Bible? A man-written book?

Well, yes, I read the Bible all the time, and I use it as a guide to help me through each day. It helps me to make decisions on things that I am unsure of because I use it to allow God to help me with it, to guide me. But I will not judge you with it, nor will I tell you what to believe. It was written by man, and a human being's words can be misused, changed, and interpreted in many different ways. Life is simple: it's love or fear, isn't it? Is it really all that hard?

You can use the name God or Jehovah or Buddha or whatever you want, but God is good. He is all the things that are just and right in this world, and he stands for love, so why not be that? Be a good person and love. Do what is right and fight for justice. If you just believe in that, how could he be prouder of you? How could he not stand you by his side as he beams his love and satisfaction with your truth? Be that!

I don't care what people think of me or how they judge me, because I can only be judged once by God. No one else has that right. Why be afraid of another human? They were created exactly the same as me and know no different from what I know of this world.

Jack had his blood transfusion, because how could I possibly deny my child any medical treatment to help save him? I didn't know any better. I believed what the professionals were saying to me, and I trusted them, as scary as that was to do.

Jack's hair now had become a nightmare. It was falling out continuously, and his pillow slip was being changed every couple of hours. It was happening so fast. Hair was everywhere. The poor kid had it all over his face, and when he turned over on his pillow, he left behind a mountain of hair.

Jack was not eating much, he must have been feeling ill if he didn't want to eat at all. Even when he did eat something small it would come straight back up. The doctors were now thinking of giving Jack nasal gastric feeds, but at this time we were going to just see how it went. He had lost weight through this ordeal, and if he didn't start eating, he would have to have the feeds.

Jack continued to have his physiotherapy, speech, and OT therapies in his room; the girls had to dress in full gowns and masks. Jack thought it was funny that the girls looked like ducks with their masks on.

"Quack, quack!" they all said together.

Soon, these hospital-based therapies would cease, because Jack would no longer be an inpatient. We would be handed over to an outside company who would come to our home and do what was necessary there. This sounded great to me, no more trekking to the hospital for short periods of time on days we had no treatment, although we had already been stuck here four nights thanks to this stupid virus.

We were all slowly getting better, and by the following day Jack had shown signs of liveliness. It would now be five nights we had been stuck in here for. He began to eat small amounts and keep it down. Anthony and Jack were getting over this virus, but I still felt off.

It was hard for Jack. He was learning to walk again, and it felt like we were going backwards with all this illness. His legs were weak without the nourishment he needed, and his body started to look slimmer and more fragile. He still went on, wanting to play and do something new and fun all the time. Luckily, he would nap well too, and so would Nansie and I. Thank goodness for coffee time!

That night, Anthony came in feeling good. Ma and Pa came in too, which made me feel good about leaving. Just before we did, the nurse came in to hook Jack up for a nasal tube feed.

"We didn't know he was having that this evening," Anthony said.

The nurse was taken aback by our surprise, even though we were fine with it, it must have shown on our faces that it had not been confirmed with us. The nurse left to double-check, and she was sure that Jack was going to start the tube feeds this evening. The dream of being able to go home tomorrow was fading away. If Jack needed to be tube-fed, we would have to give it to him at home as well.

Not more stuff to learn and do at home! How much more can we take?

The nurse made a note for someone to come in tomorrow to show me how the tube-feeding was done. I never wanted to be a nurse, but when you must do it for your baby boy, you do it. But it is scary. You don't ever want to do anything wrong or let your mind fade out while they are trying to explain things to you.

By the next morning, which was now Sunday morning, seven nights after we had arrived at emergency, Jack was so much better. He had eaten his breakfast well, and he looked great. I was so happy. The tube-feeds had been stopped for now thanks to his encouraging behaviour. We were released before midday, with no gastric feeds needed at home. Yay! We had an appointment with the dietician and for blood work on Tuesday to make sure that he was continually getting better.

When we arrived home, the first thing we did was shave Jack's head. It was something I never ever wanted to do, but with his hair just falling out in masses, it was the only thing we could do to stop it from irritating him. There he was, my little boy with his shaved head, nasal gastric tube stuck to his face, and his face droopy on his right side. There was also the indescribable unique smell of chemotherapy pouring out of his pores.

It was the first time I really saw a sick child before me. Anthony took a photo of his buzz cut, and when I got the photo processed, I realised that I could never look at it again. He looked terrible and so unwell. He was not like this to me. This photo did not show the life and energy that Jack threw out every day, or his smile and laughter. It showed a sick little boy that I could hardly recognise. I hid the photo away so that I would never have to look at it again.

CHAPTER 15

Sometimes we wonder why we come across really nasty people in our lives. One day I realised that some of the most important lessons I've learned has been because of these people. Important decisions I've made were also because of them. I didn't want to be anything like them. They taught me how it would feel to be on the other end of their ugliness, and so I did everything I could to be nothing like them. So, I guess a thank you would be appropriate. Thank you for showing me how to be kind, loving, selfless, and passionate about life and the meaning of it. Learn from these people positively. Teach them.

Anthony sat with the dietician while I played with Jack in the waiting room of the oncology ward. Jack weighed in at 11.5 kilograms, which was the lowest weight we would have liked him at. Anthony told me that the dietician had said that it was important to get him to eat foods that would help increase his body weight and energy levels.

We were to do things like add full thick cream to his food and to his milk, and not to water down his milk either. They suggested we get him eating things like potato chips and all those high-fat foods. Also, to try to get some meat into him, even if it was a mouthful of mince at a time.

I continued to feed Jack what he wanted but I was careful when he was a little vomity, giving him plain things like Jatz biscuits and potato chips. He loved eating, and when he was feeling well, he ate all the time. Jack's blood levels were looking better, and he was slowly recovering from his first round of chemotherapy and the virus.

We had six weekly check-ups on Jack's eyes, and at the moment we were doing four hours of patching a day and still continuing to place Lacri-Lube into his eye every time he went to sleep. It was great to finally have a plan and a direction so that we didn't have to be in the hospital unnecessarily. We could do more exciting things with Jack away from the hospital as everything slowly started to fall into a routine.

We enjoyed taking Jack to a little place near where we lived where there were ducks, some mean old geese, and a playground. Jack loved it! We would stand Jack on an old wooden picnic table so that he was high up, away from the huge number of birds that would attack us to get our bread.

Jack screamed continuously, while laughing, to the loud and very rude geese: "Go away! Go away!"

It was always funny, as they would nip at Poppie's bottom or secretly steal your whole piece of bread from your hands when you weren't looking. It was chaos but loads of fun. As soon as the bread was gone, so were all the ducks and geese. We were then at peace to play on the playground. It was always a nice outing for us all.

Jack would be in the hospital again this coming Friday to start another round of the major chemotherapy drugs and to have another few overnighters. It always came around so quickly, and yet the time in the hospital moved so slowly. It was hard to know what to do or where to take

Jack, because you never knew if he was going to be well enough. Plus, we had to make sure that he didn't come in contact with anyone sick. He was prone to infection. We always washed or wiped over Jack's hands just in case.

Jack wasn't feeling well again. I tried to change his nappy on the change table and saw that he was going to be sick, so I grabbed a bowl that was close to me. I made sure that I had a plastic bowl in nearly every room.

He sat up on the change table and started to vomit. I could see his nasal gastric tube slowly bulging out of his nose. I began to scream for Anthony, because I knew that if I could hold it to reinforce it, maybe I could stop the tube from coming out. I couldn't do anything to stop it, I was holding onto the bowl with one hand and Jack with the other. I just had to watch it pop in and out as he vomited.

I screamed for Anthony again, but he never came. Jack vomited again, and this time he threw the gastric tube end that was in his stomach out his mouth. It was horrifying. It was hanging out of his mouth, yet the other end was still up through his nose. With one quick swoop, without thinking, I hooked my finger into it near his nose and pulled it straight up and out. After Jack had finished, I wiped his face and slowly peeled the rest of the gastric tube from his face.

I stormed out to the lounge room with Jack and said to Anthony, "Thanks a lot for all your help!"

"What!" he said.

"I've been yelling out to you!"

"Sorry, I didn't hear ..."

"Jack's tubes came out again. I'm going to ring the hospital!"

I made the phone call and expected to be told to come in and have the tube replaced. Thankfully, because Jack didn't need any etoposide until we returned on Friday, we could just wait until then to do it. I calmed down knowing that we didn't have to make the trip back to the hospital. I think Anthony was pleased too, after my very small, little, tiny outburst. I felt like I needed ten more hands, but it's amazing how you just cope at the time.

It was Jack's cousin Lauren's fourth birthday this coming Saturday. It was a shame that we would miss it. We were due to do chemotherapy again on the Friday and stay in the hospital until Sunday. I never liked missing birthdays, especially children's birthdays, because you can never get them back. But Jack was the most important person in our lives right now, and a birthday party was small and insignificant compared to our crazy upside-down world.

Although I was sad not to go, there was also a side of me that was relieved. Everyone would be feeling sorry for us and asking us questions that we wouldn't want to answer. It was hard enough to talk about it, let alone to people we barely knew. Then we would have to watch while all the other kids jumped around happily, all healthy and full of life, while Jack sat and watched and wondered why he couldn't be just like them. I wondered what would be going on inside Jack's head.

Would he be thinking, *I used to walk and run and now I can't*. Would it make him frustrated?

Then I would start to think, *Why?* It was the biggest question with no answer. *Why Jack? Why us? Why at all?*

It was too much to bear, too much to even try to cope with while everything else was going on. There was the guilt of Jack missing out on the fun a child should be having at his age. So at least we didn't have a choice. We would be in the hospital, and we were strangely relieved. Wow, how much life had changed, that even a small child's birthday party could set off a massive wheel of different emotions, a roller coaster ride of many ups and downs.

The routine started for us again with blood work and then having to wait in the oncology ward waiting room to see Dr. Marlene after the blood results came in. The drugs started up for the day, and we started pumping the poisonous chemotherapy into Jack's tiny body.

God, are we doing the right thing? So many kids came in and out, some looking so sick. *Please God, don't let Jack look so sick.*

It was hard not to overhear some of the discussions the other parents were having with the doctors. There wasn't much privacy at all. It was embarrassing, I didn't want to show to the other parents that I could hear what was being said. I didn't want to know the disheartening stories of these children. I know that sounds harsh, but I could hardly bear Jack going through this, let alone other children and babies, the future of the world. They had never done anything to deserve such a fight. I didn't want to see them suffering. Everyone's pain became mine when I heard their stories.

There was an eighteen-month-old little baby girl who had a tumour on her kidneys. They were told that she would undergo chemotherapy first before any operation because the tumour was so big. The whole idea was to get the tumour to shrink before surgery. The conversation was that the little girl had just had a scan, and the doctors were not happy with the chemotherapy. It wasn't working. It should have reduced the tumour by now, but it had not.

The parents were told right then and there that they had booked their daughter in for surgery in two days. The shock on her mother's face! There it was again, that feeling, that instant when you realise that you are not in control. I stood there with Jack, emotionless, acting as if I could hear nothing, but my heart was just aching for them.

Please, God, make sure that you have put us all into the right hands, make sure they know what they are doing.

The nurse came to let me know that we would have to put Jack's nasal gastric tube back in again, because he was to have the etoposide the following night through it. Nansie refused to watch Jack go through it all again; it wasn't the most pleasant thing to watch, as you know. The tube was reinserted in the examination room without too much pain. Maybe he was getting used to it, but I wasn't.

We got through the day playing with cars and Play-Doh, and with all the different toys provided. Jack had a little snooze, which always gave us that small window to go and grab something to eat for ourselves, also the chance to move the car so we wouldn't get a parking fine. Yes, there was that to worry about also.

It was time to go up to the chemotherapy ward, and Anthony was with us. He always turned up about four o'clock. Anthony would carry Jack up to the ward, while I took all our belongings and the nurse wheeled Jack's drip.

He was such an amazing kid to have to go through all this and really, he didn't complain. Every now and then he would have his say, because he was sick of it all, but who wouldn't be? He wanted to run and play. He knew that it was all to help him get better, so he just accepted it. I hadn't even done that yet!

The next day, Jack vomited because of the chemotherapy drugs, and once again the nasal gastric tube came out, and once again it had to be reinserted. So now this tube was starting to really piss us off! Did we have to keep having this thing reinserted a billion times by the end of all this? I can't believe that there isn't a better way. These kids are going to vomit, and this stupid tube is going to keep coming out.

I couldn't keep watching this kid have this tube shoved down his throat another billion times. Anthony and I had decided to try to get Jack used to oral medications. He was slowly healing, so the swelling in his head should be recovering, which meant he should be feeling relief from nausea when he ate and took medication.

The tumour had been pushing on that part of his brain and now it was gone. There was just the swelling and inflammation, which would be putting pressure on it. When that healed, he would be better.

On Sunday morning, we were able to go home at around ten thirty in the morning because everything had gone to plan. There is a first time for everything. We could happily enjoy another week just to ourselves.

CHAPTER 16

The greatest power that one can own is the power of belief. Believing will create a vision that you know to be true. If you believe in yourself and your abilities, then there is nothing in this world that can stop you. The blessing is to never stop believing no matter how hard life becomes.

The outside company that helped Jack with his speech therapy, OT, and physiotherapy (which I will call WELL) had started to visit us at home. The three girls had brought lots of goodies for Jack to play with. Most of the time he was cooperative, except when he was tired. They were different girls from the ones we had at the hospital, but they were great, very patient.

We had a minor tantrum with Jack when the girls had to pack up the toys and take them back. We discussed whether there was anything they could bring along next time and leave with us, so Jack could improve on his walking and his movements. The idea was to get him a framed walker that he could use to stand upright and walk all by himself. To me, that sounded fantastic.

I was becoming bigger in my pregnancy, and it was becoming harder and harder to hold Jack up while he was walking. The strain on the back was quite difficult for anyone, but it was especially hard with a baby in the belly.

The next two weeks we were full on, with vincristine admissions on the Fridays and eye appointments, a hearing test, and a kidney function test, all of which took so much time. I had also had an appointment with my doctor for my pregnancy, which was progressing smoothly.

The kidney function test (GFR) for Jack was not one of my favourites, but I can tell you how much easier it was when you could go and walk around the hospital. Or go to the park, have lunch, eat, drink, and be merry. (It was particularly fantastic compared to the last time, when Jack had to fast and stay in one spot with his drip.)

Everything just flowed, you start to get a routine for all of your different appointments. You begin to learn what Jack likes to do and plan to do that while you are waiting, which is 90 per cent of the time. Routines started to form for each different challenge that we had to face. People began to know us by name and started to talk to us about everything. It was hard. I didn't want to talk to strangers about this.

I always acted happy, and I always looked as though nothing bothered me ... unless, of course, I was so mad that I just couldn't help it. That didn't happen often. Most of the time, I was frustrated by the system we had become entangled within, but I managed to keep it in.

I made the most of every day with Jack. I was always fine, but inside I was never fine. If someone asked me how I was, the answer would always be "Fine." I'm not stupid. A good, well-thought-out answer always made people think, "Wow, she is so strong and coping so well!" Yeah, right! All I wanted to do was hit every smiling happy person in the face.

I wanted to shut the whole system down, because to me they were just dragging out and complicating every procedure to the absolute maximum that they could. I once believed that we as human beings were so intelligent, but my world was being crushed by a system that showed me that we were complete idiots. I felt like they were always adding pressure to an already steaming pressure-cooker of a situation. Although 60 per cent of people here at least seemed to care, 40 per cent just had no idea what they were doing. That for me, wasn't good enough. I had no faith in their expertise, and I made sure that I was present at every moment anyone did anything to Jack.

I said to myself, "How do I trust the most untrustworthy?"

I thought we were to have trust in our doctors and nurses, but every day something would happen, and I no longer trusted them. I took the time to learn and understand the things they did and said, and I always questioned them if I thought that it was not correct. Most of the time, I was right. Dr. Marlene had even said to me in a previous conversation that it's always best that we as parents are standing by to make sure none of them make any mistakes. I'm not even going to comment on that one!

Jack got his walker, and it was a little different from what I thought it was going to be. Instead of it being in front of him, he held each side of it, with it going around behind him. At first, he really found it quite difficult, but like anything, once you get the hang of it, it becomes second nature to you. As Jack slowly got better at his walking, he began to zoom around the house, getting faster and faster with it. We had a few minor wall-denting issues, but it was all part of learning for him.

This would get his legs to start to strengthen up, support his weight, and control his balance. There was never a moment, though, that there wasn't somebody standing beside him. He was doing such a great job, but he was never far from a minor misjudgement or a small fall.

On our week off, Jack had to have an MRI and a lumbar puncture, which they would do both while he was under the anaesthetic.

Unless they forgot to do the lumbar puncture! God give me strength if they do.

I had asked the question in DOSA what number in line Jack would be this time. Luckily, he was first, and the proceedings ran quite smoothly. He went in around 1.30 p.m. not quite on time, but it wasn't a four o'clock disaster like the last time. He was a good boy with his fasting and he was only mildly sick when he woke in the recovery room.

The last few weeks must have gotten to me, because one morning I had decided to go out with Nansie, Poppie and Jack, but before I left I went to the toilet and found that I was bleeding. Fear completely took over. I rang my private hospital, and I was told to come straight in. Nansie and Poppie dropped me off while they took Jack back home; there was no need for him to be around another hospital.

I rang Anthony, and he was going to finalise a few things at work and then come in. You know, no one really seemed to be worried or be too concerned at all ... except me! Maybe that was their plan to keep me calm, who knows.

I was sent up to the maternity ward, where they put monitors on my belly to listen to the baby's heartbeat. I lay there calm, cool, and collected, and I continued to mildly bleed. I was just over six months pregnant, and although my exterior was calm, inside I was upset.

Thousands of questions zoomed through my head, horrible thoughts of what could happen. *How will I cope? I can't have this happening, not now. It was just too much!*

I was feeling like no one had any urgency about it, not even Anthony. He was being so calm over the phone, "It will be fine, don't worry."

Sure, don't worry!

I did remember that my friend Sarah had a mild bleed like this with her first pregnancy, and all was well. That made me feel a little better about the situation.

Breathe ... breathe.

Anthony came in after they had monitored the baby for a while, and it was starting to look like the baby was going to be fine. I got a jab in the arm, and afterwards I realised that it was a jab I never needed. It was a precautionary injection for my negative blood type, but after going to all the effort to find out that Anthony's blood was a perfect match with mine, the precautionary jab was never needed.

Awesome, there goes the trust again! Oops, the doctor didn't check my notes properly, but don't worry, it will have no effect. Yeah, thanks! If I had known why I was getting injected, I could have questioned it. But I trusted them. I was in a stressful position and I trusted them.

After two hours of monitoring, I was sent home. I was starving. We grabbed some fried chicken on the way. I could see the sign from my hospital room, and it had been calling me for the whole time. Just another minor battle over and done with. The baby was healthy and so was I, thank goodness.

Two days after that it was Friday again. Which meant it was time for Jack to have the next round of chemotherapy. This was the third round.

How will it be this time? I wondered.

We went in and had blood work at nine thirty in the morning. I loved being one of the first ones in there, because you rarely had to wait, and if you did it wouldn't be for long. Next, we would walk around or have a coffee for an hour and then go down to the clinic, where we would wait for the blood results to come in.

Jack's blood results looked good, so he was a go-ahead for his third round of chemotherapy. Surprisingly, the weekend went very well, much the same as before. Jack was still vomiting and lethargic, but he would have his bursts of energy and fun times. We got through this round so much better than the others. We left in the morning on Sunday. We had all the medications we needed, and you couldn't have gotten us out of there fast enough.

The next week went unbelievably well, with his eye appointment going quickly and the same outcome of patching as much as we could, with a possibility of Jack needing glasses further down the track. Jack's Friday appointment for his vincristine chemotherapy flew past, maybe I was getting a handle on this. We were only in the hospital from 10:30 a.m. to 2:15 p.m. blood work and all.

The WELL girls came to see us again, and this time the physiotherapist explained to me that Jack might benefit from wearing braces on his legs. I actually thought that he had come such a long way in learning to walk again. Even though he was still unstable on his feet, the walker was helping.

The physiotherapist explained that Jack's muscles were quite tight and that braces would help to stretch them and assist his walking further. She also taught me how to exercise and stretch his muscles myself.

I was slightly saddened by the thought of Jack in leg braces, and even having to sleep in them. I don't know why; I felt like he already had enough to cope with. The list just kept on growing and growing. It was so hard to cope with everything, not just for him but for me too.

That sounds so selfish. I can't believe I just said that. Who cares if I'm finding it a little hard? Oh, you poor thing, at least I didn't have my head sliced open and everything I once knew completely taken away from me in an instant.

I just wanted him to be that little boy I brought into the hospital. I wanted him to have some normality, but I felt like that was getting further and further away from us.

When Jack got to his week off of this cycle, it was surprising that he continued to vomit throughout it. Usually that subsided, and this week was also the week he no longer needed to have the etoposide. I was worried, but maybe his body was just trying to deal with all the drugs.

I had an appointment this week for a scan for the baby, I had to wait for the results. It was a relief to know that the baby was doing well after having the bleed. Although it was very stressful having the scan and waiting, it was great to hear that the baby was doing perfectly.

Jack's vomiting finally eased up. We headed in now for Jack's fourth cycle of chemotherapy. We did his blood work, waited, and did everything as we normally did, ending up once again at the clinic. When Dr. Marlene spoke to us this time it was a different. Jack's blood levels were not high enough for him to continue with his treatment. He had neutropenia, which meant that his neutrophils in his white blood cells were too low; his body needed them to fight off bacteria and other infections.

The hardest thing was that it was best for him to be away from other people, especially other children, as children are good at carrying all sorts of infections. Jack loved to see his friends and family, but if they were in anyway unwell then we couldn't be in contact with them.

I wasn't sure if I was disappointed or relieved. It meant that we went straight back home, bags and all. We would wait until the following Friday and try again. I had hoped that Jack wouldn't be in hospital or on etoposide over Christmas. By the calendar, even with this little hiccup, it was still looking good for that to happen.

It was so nice having another week all to ourselves, going out and not worrying about hospitals, appointments, or any sort of poisonous drugs. Jack started to look healthier. You don't realise how sick your son is looking from his treatment. It's a very slow process, so to you as a mother, he always looks the same. He looked just like Jack, my son. I didn't realise that to other people, friends, family, even strangers, he was looking ill. This extra week gave him a little more energy, more colour in his face, and a great deal more life. It made me wonder if what we were doing was best for Jack. But I didn't know what else to do.

The week went by quickly, and it was a nice time to have. Once again, we made our way back to the hospital, where we started our routine. Nansie always came in with me, which was wonderful; she drove us in, so I could always sit in the back with Jack just in case he wasn't feeling well. She was also able to move the car during the day, because there were only ever two-hour parks to be found around the hospital. Which in my opinion is ridiculous!

We went to the clinic, where we waited for Dr. Marlene. She called us in, and it was not what we were expecting again. Jack's blood levels were still not high enough. Jack still had neutropenia, with his neutrophils lower than 1.0. I was a little worried now. Jack could get very ill or catch a virus that would send him into hospital for an indefinite period of time. The dates were getting a little too close to Christmas. Would we possibly be in hospital? Or would Jack be on the horrid etoposide? That would be fine, of course, but I just wanted it to be somewhat normal. Was it wrong to wish for a normal Christmas? So home again we went.

This week did not flow as well as the last. We had a few appointments that filled up the days. I had another appointment with my obstetrician, which all went well. It was just the hour wait that pips you, I felt like all I ever did was wait around.

This week also, we had to go into the city to a different hospital to discuss Jack's radiotherapy, which was slowly creeping up on us. After this last round of chemotherapy, Jack would have to undergo six to eight weeks of radiotherapy. Sometimes I felt like things were contradictory, like being told that radiotherapy would not be done on any children under the age of three, yet here we are with a two-year-old getting prepared for six to eight whole weeks of radiotherapy. Even the amount just sounded insane: forty sessions.

There were so many questions going around in both Anthony's and my head. We had written a few of them down, because it was something that we didn't know too much about. We had been told different things by many different people who gave us a basic knowledge. We had asked several different nurses and doctors about whether Jack's hair would grow back in the large patch at the back of his head that would have the radiotherapy. Every single one of them told me yes, which was positive. It just might be thinner or darker or even curly, which would be quite funny, when it did grow back.

We got to the radiotherapy hospital a little bit early, and we did not take Jack in with us, as it was a chance for us to have a clear chat with the doctor. While we were in there, we were greeted by a lovely young man who was going to go through a few things with us before we went in to see the doctor. The strange thing was that Anthony already knew him; they both had worked at the same department store when they were younger. It was such a nice surprise to have someone you knew and could trust.

We asked him a whole bunch of questions before we even got into the doctor. We asked whether Jack's hair would grow back where the radiotherapy would be done, and this young man just came straight out with...no.

The thing was that we had asked so many people, and they had all told us yes, but he simply said no. He explained the radiotherapy, how it was a beam of radiation that was measured precisely at many different directions.

It would kill off cells in Jack's brain in one area only, which had been measured and given exact coordinates. That would cause a mild burn on Jack's skin, just like a sunburn.

The mild short-term effects would be things like nausea, tiredness, and skin irritations, but it was the long-term effects we were worried about most of all. The long-term effects in children could be greater because we were zapping a brain that was nowhere near finished developing. There could be learning difficulties through school, where Jack might need help, such as tutoring. There could be memory loss, stunted growth and development, and I there was always the chance of reoccurrence too.

Once again, the cure could end up being the culprit!

Things always got worse just when we thought we had prepared ourselves for the absolute worst. We realised that we hadn't even taken the topping off the cake yet. Thinking of the worst-case scenarios helped us to never be surprised. It got us used to dealing with things before they even happened. The problem was, the worst we were thinking wasn't even the beginning. That's when the whole system starts to fail.

There was also talk about how close the beam would get to the nerves of the eyes and ears. If there was any huge chance of deterioration, they would contact us, and we could discuss it further. There was so much, so much that could damage Jack, but we still agreed to continue with it after all these negative outcomes that could occur because it was worth the cancer not coming back.

Oh wait, that's right. Another one of the effects was that it might cause secondary cancers to arise. Yes, this whole process to stop the cancer could turn around and cause cancer. We are so stupid! Again, we were being guided to follow this process to do all that was possible to obtain Jack's survival, but it could also make him worse.

We had to try. How could we not try? It would be like giving up on him ... for me, anyway. If he was alive, then all the small mountains of things that could happen to him that we could conquer together were worth it in the end, if he was to be cured. At this moment, that was true, but this poor child would have so much suffering. He had suffered so much already, it seemed as though he hadn't even begun.

There was some preparation for the radiotherapy that Jack had to go through. He went under some mild anaesthetic so that they could make a mask of his face. I'm unsure of how they did it, but the time went by quickly, so it must have been quite easy. Every time he would have radiotherapy, they would put this mask on him with an oxygen mask over the top for the forty radiotherapy procedures. It was just another thing we got through to make sure everything went smoothly when the day came for him to have his radiotherapy.

CHAPTER 17

The fear of eating a cake will kill you long before eating the cake itself. Fear creates poison. Love creates healing. Enjoy life to the fullest allowing yourself a treat every now and then. Have fun. Do all things with the act of love and not the act of fear and the rewards will be overwhelming.

Before we knew it, Jack was up for another Friday in the clinic. We had the blood work done, and it was quite busy today. We sat next to a young boy who was about ten-years-old who was having treatment as well. We happened to get into a conversation with his family about a camp for kids with cancer that most of the children having treatment had been to. The conversation then went into how most of them went home because of an outbreak of chicken pox at the camp. They thought that their son might have contracted it, but he was showing no symptoms. He was having his blood work done for his treatment but also to see if he had any infections or viruses.

Oh my God!

There was a boy sitting next to us who could possibly be contaminated with chicken pox, and Jack had just had two weeks of having neutropenia! His chance of getting any illness was mega high, there was so much flying through my head. It was close to Christmas, and he could be severely ill. This could be huge, even to the point that he was unrecoverable.

We were called in next for bloods, and I was up within a second and out of there. It was too late. My mind now was in overdrive because there was more to worry about. I couldn't stop the banter telling me that something bad could happen from this.

We went through all the usual stuff and found that Jack's bloods were good to go. I discussed my conversation about the boy who had the chicken pox with Dr. Marlene, but she was positive that Jack would be all right. For some reason, I believed the things she told me, and I was a great deal more relaxed about it.

Dr. Marlene was the only one who, when I looked at her, made me feel like she knew exactly what she was talking about. There were no stumbles and no doubts. We started the final chemotherapy for this four-cycle round, and all went through exactly the same. It would work out that Jack would be on the etoposide for Christmas. Anthony came in the afternoon, and around five o'clock we trotted Jack up to the ward where we would settle in.

Jack had a bad day the next day with his vomiting. We tried to keep food and fluids to a minimum, because too much would make him so sick. The day was a hard one, and during it Jack had a reaction to one of the medications he was given. The drug, as we knew it, was called Maxolon. It was given alternately with ondansetron, which helped with Jack's nausea.

Here comes a question, he'd been vomiting all day; did it really work? Was it making him feel any better at all? If it was working in some way, then I hate to think how he would have been feeling without it! Maxolon was inserted very slowly through his IV, which went through his port. The nurse was finalising it when Nansie and I noticed Jack's face. It was just emotionless, like a statue. His eyes widened a little, and the nurse left.

I looked at him and called his name. "Jack, Jack ... are you all right?"

There was nothing from him at all. He just sat on the bed staring in front of himself. I grabbed him and shook him a little, looking into his eyes. "*Jack!*"

He vaguely looked at me. He was angry at me, and slowly said, "What?"

"Are you okay?" I asked him again. He just nodded his head to say yes as he lay down on the bed.

"That's not right!" Nansie said to me, and I agreed.

Jack fell asleep, and I don't know if it was the drugs or if he was so tired and exhausted from not eating and vomiting that he just had to rest. Nansie and I had our little cry over it. It was all so emotional. We told the nurses what happened, and Jack was taken off Maxolon immediately.

I think Nansie and I only just made it through the day. At the end, when Anthony turned up at the hospital, I lifted Jack up because he had been sitting on me for quite a while. I noticed that Jack had wet right through his nappy. I was wet all over my thighs and all the way down to my crotch. Worried I went straight into the room's bathroom and had a shower. The thought of chemotherapy on my skin and running down my crotch was bad, I was pregnant. It scared me to have the poison anywhere near me, but it was *on* me.

I scrubbed and scrubbed to make sure that I got it all off. It was nice to have a hot shower after such a huge day, and it was so much more comfortable being able to do what you needed to do privately in your own room. I was so thankful for that. Small mercies.

My thoughts sometimes were quite weird to me. I was scared that I had gotten Jack's urine on me. I dealt with it the best way I could at the time, and I stopped worrying about it. My thoughts should have been concern for my little baby who had not yet entered the world, but instead I was worried about that moment. I couldn't worry about the future, only that moment.

I had to worry for Jack, and I had to get the job done, which was Jack. It sometimes made me feel guilty that I didn't worry more about my little one not yet here, but what was the point in worrying when there was no way of knowing if anything would happen from being exposed to chemotherapy? It wasn't just this time but for the whole process with Jack. There weren't going to be people around me every second of the day, so I would be exposed to chemotherapy many times while I was pregnant. One thing at a time. That's the only way you can get through anything in life. One thing, just one.

I remember when I was younger, I made up this rule that when something bad or hard happened in my life, I would tell myself, *Tarina, tomorrow or in one week, this problem will no longer be here, and once again, you will be just fine. This will pass, and even though right now it's hard, soon it will be over.*

Jack's case was a little different. This wasn't going to be over in a day or a week. It was going to be a long time if ever for this to be all right for Jack and for us. It was important to just get each appointment, or chemotherapy treatment, or blood test, or MRI over and done with one at a time. I had to soak up every moment that we weren't at hospital and be happy that we were together, just playing and having fun.

This moment was having a shower to wash off any chemotherapy and then just get back to the task at hand, and that was loving and cuddling Jack while he was feeling unwell. We made it through another hospital stay and returned home. Jack had been a little more lethargic this round. We would count this one as a hard one, but right now, Nansie and I were home, and home was good.

Jack continued to vomit a great deal more this week compared to the other times. It was so unpredictable. There was a moment when we went to Ma and Pa's house for dinner. Anthony's parents had invited Brenton and Kerry and their two daughters, Lauren and Ashley, over too. We weren't really thrilled about going because Jack just had so much medication that he had to take and giving him the etoposide at night as well as being out was going to be hard. But we wanted desperately to be normal and we wanted Jack to go out and see his family.

By now, we had developed a well-devised plan for Jack to take the etoposide orally. That's right! That stupid tube had been vomited out one too many times, and Anthony and I had refused to return Jack to the hospital to have it reinserted. Instead, we decided to try Jack with it orally, and it worked. We would syringe it down one side of his mouth and then shove a bottle of milk in his mouth straight after, and then a chocolate. It actually started to work so well we all became etoposide experts.

Although most times Jack was great with it, sometimes he wasn't. It was like having a world of stress to pack with you to just go to dinner with family for the night. The reason we went to Ma and Pa's that night is because we wanted things to be normal, just like they used to be. Jack had missed out on so much already. Play with his two cousins sounded like a nice thing for him to do. It was so hard, always watching Jack and making sure he wouldn't fall and hurt himself, but he had a great time.

When it got to the time for Jack to have his etoposide, the stress for both Anthony and I was huge, but we had planned his ondansetron (anti-vomit) perfectly so that it would have the best chance at working before giving him the etoposide. We locked ourselves in a bedroom armed with the etoposide, gloves, our yellow disposal bin for the syringe, and a vomit bowl. If he vomited it out straight away, we would have to leave for home so that we could readminister it.

Jack was not interested at all in having his medication that night. He was having a great time with the girls and he didn't want to stop. Anthony was getting a bit stressed with it all, I could tell, but we tried our best at being normal for one night. It didn't work. Jack vomited straight away within a second, and so we had to leave to readminister the drug when we got home.

"I can't do this!" I said to Anthony as we drove off in the car. "It's just too hard!"

"I know!" he said. "We have got to stay home when he's on etoposide. We can't take it everywhere. It's just too hard and stressful for us."

We agreed that there would be no more outings at night-time when Jack was on etoposide. How could we have thought that we could do it? It was too hard even at home, but Jack had a great time, and that was a good thought.

It was time for blood work again, and this week we had to give Jack his vincristine. An MRI had been planned, which went as well as could be expected. We also had an appointment with our neurosurgeon, who had conducted the operation that removed Jack's tumour. The neurosurgeon was pleased with the MRI results. They did show some mild scar tissue, but the doctor did not seem worried. Everything appeared normal and on the right track.

The following Friday was quite interesting. After Jack had his blood work done, we went into the clinic as normal for his vincristine. We were sent straight through to start it instead of seeing Dr. Marlene first. She would come out and see us later.

I was still worried about Jack being on etoposide over Christmas after our last episode. He had been looking flatter than normal this week while his vomiting continued. Jack was laying on one of the beds when Dr. Marlene came over to me to discuss Jack's blood results. Apparently, they were good except for something called his ANC, which I am sure she was referring to his neutrophil count again. It was as low as 0.16, which wasn't good.

"What are we going to do?" I asked.

Dr. Marlene said to me, "Jack will have his vincristine today, but we will just take him off of the etoposide for the rest of this round."

No more Etoposide this round!!!!! YEEE-HAAAAA!!!!! Merry Christmas Jack!

"You mean I don't have to give him the rest of his etoposide at all?"

"No," she confirmed. "We will just leave it for now. No more etoposide for this cycle. He is going to go on pentamidine today, which is a different type of antibiotic. This is going to take over from the Bactrim you have been giving him, just in case it has been affecting his lower blood levels."

She paused and then continued. "So, no more etoposide and no more Bactrim, but he will be here a bit longer today because the pentamidine takes about an hour to go through. I want one more blood check before Christmas, too, just to check how they are tracking. I want you to watch out for any fevers as well, and if he does get one, you know to bring him straight into emergency."

"I understand. No worries at all!" I said.

"The pentamidine will be run on a cycle also, so that will be every three weeks he will need that."

I smiled and nodded and wished her a very Merry Christmas. I looked at Nansie and smiled. "No more etoposide this round!"

"Thank God!" she said.

This may sound crazy, but that was one of the best things I could have ever heard. Jack was not going to be on any chemotherapy over Christmas. What a present! It was going to be a hard Christmas anyway, but this was a dream come true. The stress levels would go right down, and we could do our very best at making this a fun and happy time for Jack. I was worried about the fact that Jack could get a fever and have to come back into the hospital ... but we would deal with that if it happened.

While we were in the clinic that day, the toy therapist gave all the kids a Christmas present. Jack was given a big farm grader, which kept him entertained for most of the day.

We had to be moved up to the chemotherapy ward for his pentamidine, as they were making arrangements for the clinic to be repainted and recarpeted. There were about six of us in the big double room in the ward having treatment. It was a little awkward and very squishy, but nothing was downing me today.

We left by one in the afternoon, which was a record time for us, even with an added hour on top of what we normally would do. I think they needed us out as soon as possible so that all the arrangements for the renovations to the clinic could go ahead. Isn't it amazing how quickly things can get done when they have a time limit? It just shows how things could run. That ended our four months of chemotherapy. Four by four weekly rounds completed. The next step was the radiotherapy for forty sessions, and then it would be four by eight weekly rounds of chemotherapy.

CHAPTER 18

A gift can come in any size, shape, or form. It can come wrapped big or small. But it is the meaning behind the gift that holds all of the magic. A piece of paper given to a loved one as a gift that states upon it how much they are loved is worth far more than a diamond bracelet given to impress.

The next blood work was done just before Christmas, and all was looking positive. Jack had slowly become better in himself, and the vomiting was gradually stopping. It was time now to think about having some fun with Jack and opening a bucket load of presents.

We had Christmas Eve at our house so that the whole family could accommodate to Jack and how he would be feeling during the night. It was hard to see him watching the kids while he sat on the floor. His balance while sitting was improving, and his walking was slowly progressing every day, but he was still wonky. Yes, of course, he had his moments, my poor little man. Sometimes I thought that it was too much for him, but he was having a great time. I think he just needed to slow down and rest every now and then to recuperate.

Santa Claus had come overnight and left Jack an electric 6-volt Mud Warrior Jeep. Although Jack was still a little bit grumpy and not too interested in the Jeep, we went with the flow of what he wanted to do. By the time we got to Nansie's house at eight that morning to do the massive opening of presents, Jack was in the mood to drive that Jeep right up the street to her house.

Nansie's backyard was big, and he enjoyed learning how to drive it, both in forward and in reverse. There was the usual crowd there for Christmas morning: Nansie, Poppie, Poppie's sister Linda, and my brother Shane's family. His wife Kerry and daughter Joey. Anthony's sister Leanne (Aunty Lally) and her boyfriend, Dave, were there too. We all made our own breakfast and coffees and chose a seat in the lounge room near the Christmas tree full of presents. There was a beautiful blue wooden chair and table set by the tree, which was for Jack from Nansie. He just loved it! It was a great place for him to sit and suck on some milk and open those presents.

It was time for the first one, and of course, we let Jack have the honours. It chose a present from Aunty Lally and Uncle Dave, they were always very good at choosing just the right presents for everyone, and this time they got it too right. It was a big truck full of little cars. A carry case to hold all his Matchbox cars in. Well, Jack thought it was amazing, and all he wanted to do was open it right then and there and play with it. The problem was that he had no interest in any other presents that came his way.

Thanks a lot, Aunty Lally, just go right ahead and steal the show why don't you! Oh, and thank you too, Uncle Dave. Better not leave you out.

After a short time passed, we had a break, so Jack and Joey could have a run around and a drive in the Jeep again. Jack was driving that thing all the way up the edge of Nansie's grass, onto her rocks and back down again.

He was getting the hang of this. Joey loved it too. She was almost eight years old, and she thought it was awesome. We hung on to some of Jack's presents and spread them throughout the day so that it wasn't all too much for him at once.

We went home for a while; Jack was exhausted and had a sleep on the couch. When he woke up, we went back to Nansie's for lunch. Jack had a small crystal port glass with his apple juice in it, so he could do a cheers with everybody. He thought he was so grown up. Pa came to lunch at Nansie's also, and then after we had filled our bellies, we went home to play with all the toys Jack had received.

Pa came back to our house for a little bit of playtime with Jack, who was blown away by how much stuff he got. I think we just really wanted to spoil him this year because of all that had happened. It had been a great day, and it had turned out just as wonderful as I had hoped for.

Anthony's birthday is two days after Christmas, and this time I had bought the two of us some tickets to the fancy Gold Class movies. This is where you can watch a movie and have your feet up the whole time while you eat and drink. I was a little worried while I was watching the movie. You know those thoughts you have.

If I go into labour, I will just slowly walk out of here. But what if my water breaks all over this chair? Yuck!

I still had four and a half weeks to go, and Jack was a late one, so I ended up forgetting about all those silly things you think about and just enjoyed the movie.

A couple of days later, which was the Sunday exactly four weeks before I was due, I woke up at seven in the morning desperate to go to the toilet. I did, and I had accidentally wet myself ... or so I thought. After Anthony rescued me with a new pair of underwear, I wet myself again.

That's weird! I thought.

Every now and then I just let go without even knowing I was doing it. I couldn't even get off the toilet, and then I realised my water had just broken, or it was leaking ... *Oh my God!*

"Honey!" I yelled out. "I think we are having a baby today! My water just broke!"

"No way! Are you kidding?"

"No!" I said. "We are about to have a baby, and I cannot get off this toilet."

Anthony rang the hospital, and he rang Nansie so that she could take care of Jack for us. Anthony would stay in hospital with me that night and then come home to take care of Jack. I was a little nervous with the whole birth thing again and taking care of a new baby, but you just, once again, take it as it comes.

CHAPTER 19

Everyone sees God differently. I can see God in all of us, even in those who say they do not believe, because they act so close to love that even without knowing, they are teaching God to those around them. Teach to others that it's so much more fun being happy and helping others than trying to suck as much as you can from everyone and everything around you for your own personal gain. Don't squash people on the way up, instead love them, so that when you are on the way down, they will catch you and hold you up high on their shoulders, because they want to. This is God. This is teaching God to others. He is Love.

· ❤ · ❤ · ❤ · ❤ · ❤ ·

We went into the private hospital where I was going to have the baby, and I sat in the reception area where the nurses sat. They showed me to a recliner to rest in while they had my room cleaned. I was given scones and a cup of tea, which eased my hungry belly. Don't worry, I shared some with Anthony.

I had just thought about the date, which was December 30. I really hoped that this baby came today and not tomorrow. One of my good friends was born on New Year's Eve, and she hated it! Everyone seemed to forget her or think that her birthday was actually January 1.

I used to tease her and say, "How could your parents be so inconsiderate, planning you on such a day?"

Now here I was doing the same thing. I couldn't believe that this little one had come so early. I hoped that meant that its whole life, it would be early. We got to our room, and to my surprise, the midwife I had was the same one I had when Jack was born. She was amazing. I felt comfortable and was not in any real pain at all.

The time ticked on. I saw my obstetrician, Dr. L. and she thought the best idea would be to wait and try a natural birth. I had to have antibiotics pumped through me because my water had broken; it was to stop any infections that could occur. It was a very long day. The bed I had in the room was a delivery bed, which was unbelievably hard, so most of the day, I sat on one of the single chairs in the room. If nothing were to happen, I would have a C-section at around eleven the next morning. Yes, that's right, New Year's Eve. Great!

My midwife had requested that my bed be changed to a more comfortable one because the labour beds were apparently not for sleeping on, but we never saw it. The bed I was on was just so unbearably hard that I made Anthony get off of his rickety old fold-out, and I went on that instead. It was only mildly better.

I had some large contractions during the night, but nothing that even made me whimper, and I eventually fell asleep. In the morning, when my wonderful midwife returned, she was cross that I had not had my bed swapped over. The replacement bed had been sitting in the hallway right by my room door the whole night. All the nurses had to do was wheel it in for me, it never happened. If I knew that it was there I would have gone and got the thing myself!

Dr. L. returned that morning, and still nothing had happened. I was told that I had a lazy uterus and that I would be sent down for a C-section shortly. Dr. L. went through the complications and told me that because there was not much fluid left in the baby's sack, there was a possibility that the baby could get nicked when she made the C-section incision.

"No, there won't be!" just came flying right out of my mouth. "Because you are going to be very, very careful so that doesn't happen."

She just smiled and replied, "Of course."

I don't need any more shit in my life lady! Do your job with no mistakes!

They put me onto a new bed, and *ow!* my butt was so sore that it felt so good on the soft mattress. The nurses got me ready in my sexy hospital attire and rolled me down to theatre. This is where I started to get nervous. The only thing I hated was the massive needle in your back to numb you from the waist down. It was indescribable, the feeling of it going into your spine, and although it probably only took a minute, I swear that it was the worst part about the whole birth thing. It's not that it hurts, it just feels weird and wrong. I hated it!

So, there I was sitting hunched over, grabbing onto Anthony's hands tightly as the anaesthetist slowly tried to get this needle into my spine. After the third attempt he was still not able to do it. I was freaking out! Why, for the one thing you hate getting done, can they not get it right ... why? On the fifth go, he got it, thank God. He nearly got a needle in his eye ball if he had taken any longer!

We knew with Jack that we were having a boy, but with this baby we decided to let it be a surprise. The doctors started everything up, and I was feeling so very gooooood at this moment. Then we heard it: the screaming of a new baby.

"It's a boy!" the doctors cried.

Anthony and I were just smiling, and I began to cry. It must have seemed unusual, because everyone asked if I was all right. I was at peace. I saw our new little boy, who looked just the opposite of Jack. He was so much plumper, even though he was five weeks earlier than Jack and his nose ... well, I think he got my long, big, straight nose. It was hard to miss. He was gorgeous.

But sadly, there was one thing I started to think, *If God gave me another boy, was he giving me a gift because he knew that Jack would not survive this? Does this mean that Jack won't be cured?*

Why do we think these stupid things in our heads? Maybe it was just all the drugs at the time, I don't know. All I knew was that my new baby was absolutely magnificent!

We named him Luke. I loved the name Luke, and although Anthony wanted to call him Riley, we agreed just at that moment that his first name was Luke. He was a strong, healthy boy, and Luke was perfect for him. He was a really good baby, and when Jack came in to see him for the first time, Jack just fell in love.

"A baby!" Jack said as he held his brother and stroked Luke's face. He didn't want to let the baby go.

Jack was so gentle with Luke, and even though he needed a small reminder every now and then that it was very important to be careful with the baby, Jack was otherwise gentle. He would show us where Luke's eyes and ears were and so on. Jack went back home with Nansie for another night while Anthony helped me out with the new baby. Although Luke was a good sleeper, it was me who couldn't get a single minute's sleep because of the little noises he would make.

It's funny how you have to wait for all the natural motherly instincts to kick in again. I knew he was all right with all these noises he was making, but I found myself continually looking over and checking him. Plus, we had messages all night because it was New Year's, of course, and so we had many congratulations on our phones after midnight.

The next day, I was able to have a shower and get up on my feet. I was excited about getting my morning tea and lunch and all the other meals brought in to me, just like a hotel. I tried to catch up on some sleep every now and then but found that you always had someone popping in on you. Anthony went home to check on Jack.

I remember my paediatrician for Luke coming in and telling me that Luke was doing really well. My new paediatrician was highly recommended, and yes, he was lovely. There was a small patch like a birthmark on the back-right side of Luke's head. As the doctor explained to me, it was a group of cells that hadn't formed correctly, hair would not grow from this mark properly. Luke would have to go to a specialist for it, and it might have to be removed later in life. It was a form of cancer.

Cancer!!!!!

My eyes grew, and he could see that I was starting to freak out. He stopped me, by saying, "It's fine, it's a benign type which is very, very common, and it's not in the same field as Jack's. It's just what they call it because it is a group of cells."

"So, what do I do?" I asked, trying not to cry.

"It's fine, and maybe when he is older, before puberty, he may need it cut out. Very minimal; there is no need at to worry at all. I see a little boy who has them all over his head, and his hair covers all of them up completely."

I looked at him, and I think that I was comfortable with it. He seemed genuine that it was not much to worry about, and even though it had a dreaded C-word attached, it was not the same as Jack's. It was more like a birthmark.

After being in the hospital for four days, I could go to a five-star hotel for two nights with Luke, which I thought would be something different. The hospital had a few rooms there and a room for a nurse, so you were cared for all the time. The bed was a king-size, the bathroom was beautiful, and the food was awesome. You were allowed free meals and a choice of entrée, main, and dessert for lunch and dinner. There was so much good food that Anthony could have some too. I'll share!

Radiotherapy had started mid-week this week for Jack, and even though little Luke had come into this world four weeks early, it was a small blessing because it worked in with Jack's radiotherapy perfectly.

The plan from now on was that every Sunday night, Anthony and Pa, would go into the chemotherapy ward at the specialist hospital to have Jack's port accessed with the butterfly needle, this needle stayed in the whole week of treatment. This was done so the anaesthetic could be put straight through it, for the radiotherapy. Then Anthony would take Jack in early in the morning to the radiotherapy hospital in the city, from Monday to Friday, to have his radiotherapy treatment. They would take the butterfly needle out on Friday.

Anthony would wake Jack up, quickly dress him, and get him into the car half asleep so that he had no time to think about eating and drinking. Then straight to the radiotherapy hospital, where he would play for a small amount of time with a ball he had become fond of from their toy box. Then down the hall to the room with the big machine.

The walls in the rooms were all decked out with beautiful and colourful paintings, which made everything brighter and not so dreary. The team had made Jack a beautiful poster of the days to count down: forty in total. He could place a sticker of one of the characters from the movie *Cars*, which he loved, onto the poster each day he had his treatment.

He would be put under the anaesthetic and then the mask that had been made especially for him previously, to keep him perfectly still, was placed over his face with an oxygen mask over that. I know that this was tough for Anthony; I don't know how I would have been to see him like that. Anthony took photos, and to this day they are hard for me to look at. I suppose that when each day went past, it became like a routine to them both, making it in a small way easier to cope with.

When the procedure was all over, which was only about fifteen minutes, Jack would go to recovery. Anthony would place a chocolate frog and a bottle of milk in front of him as he slowly awoke. Jack would shovel them down and was all right with it, no vomiting.

Jack and Anthony came in to visit for the first day I was at the hotel, and we decided that we would all stay the night. It was nice to catch up and talk about how the first days of radiotherapy were going. The bed was big enough for all of us to sleep in. I had not yet had more than about seven hours sleep total in the first four nights, and I was so tired. Luke was feeding every three hours. He was getting back to sleep after the feeds, but

I just couldn't sleep with all his noises, and everything else that was going around in my head.

That night, it was hard work getting Jack to sleep in a different place. I had gotten up quietly throughout the night to feed Luke without disrupting them both. It was midnight and I still couldn't get Luke back to sleep again. I was so tired that I could hardly stand, then Anthony awoke and noticed that I was struggling. He got up and took over for me.

The nurse came in while Anthony was trying to rock Luke back to sleep, and I was lying on the bed. I asked for some paracetamol for my back, which had been causing me pain and agony, more than what my surgery had. I just began to sob.

You know when you say to people, "Man, I'm so exhausted!" Well, at that moment, I knew the true meaning of exhaustion: when you can no longer speak because there is no energy left. It took me a few good minutes to even gain enough energy to raise my left arm to my mouth to take the tablets. It was scary.

The nurse was so lovely. She said, "I am going to take Luke for the next two hours, just so you can get some rest. Then I will bring him back for his next feed. How does that sound?"

Anthony handed Luke over to her, and Jack had not even moved with all the commotion going on. I fell asleep. At two in the morning, the nurse returned, and I was a new person. It was the first night I actually got two hours sleep in a row. I had energy, and my back felt so much better. The old me was back, and I hoped that I never had that feeling again. It was not normal and a little freaky, having no control at all, just unable to move.

We decided that the next night, it would be better if we left Jack in his normal environment. Anthony and Jack visited after radiotherapy and then went home again. It was nice that they told me all about it. I was missing out on a huge part of Jack's therapy, but I knew what a great dad he had, and it was my duty now to take care of Luke. It wouldn't be long, and we would be home all together as a family. Things would be able to get into some routine, one that involved sleeping, I hoped.

I found myself at first scared of being alone with Luke, but this was the first night and day that I felt able to rest and get on top of things. I had a long hot shower as Luke slept in his little wheelie crib by the door, so I could hear him. I napped during the day while he slept. I was filling my belly with awesome food and starting to feel strong and confident.

The following day, the stitches came out, and it was time to go home. Anthony picked me up, and when we put Luke into the car seat ... oh my God! He was so tiny! Such a precious little thing just oohing and goo-ing all the time. I think the family was scared to touch him because he was so small. Luke was a great baby. We never had many hard times with him. He had to go in his own room which was right next to ours, because the little noises that he made were cute, but they kept me awake.

The third night at home, Jack woke early in the morning with a horrible croupy cough. It brought me to tears hearing him, it sounded so painful. Anthony called Nansie, and they both took Jack to the hospital while I stayed home with Luke. It was only a couple of hours before they returned. We were to give Jack the dexamethasone again, which was the steroid that reduced inflammation, it would help around the voice box. Apparently, the cough sounded much worse than it was, and in a few days, Jack would be fine. And he was.

Jack continued his radiotherapy. Anthony took him every day while I stayed home with Luke to feed him and do all the other stuff you do with a newborn (sleep). Each day's trip in for radiotherapy had turned into a novelty for Jack because all the people dealing with him made it special. It was like an outing.

We went out on a real outing one day and took Jack to look at beds. We found the coolest car bed; he loved it, and so we got it. Jack had been sleeping between us, which made us feel safe together, but squishy. He had outgrown his cot, and this was a great opportunity for us to give him something special and seriously cool. Jack loved it and slept in it instantly, which freed up our bed and gave Jack something to look forward to.

Jack's hair had started to grow back nicely. As the radiotherapy treatment continued, the back of his head began to get redder and redder, which was normal. We just had to apply a special moisturiser to it a few times a day. It was no trouble. The hair was not growing there, not that I expected it to during the radiotherapy treatment. But you always have that hope that his hair is so strong that it will just grow anyway. Of course, it didn't.

During this time of Jack's radiotherapy, it was his cousin Ashley's birthday. The party was going to be held at a park, which sounded lovely. It was the first time we felt confident in taking Jack out to a family function. He hadn't vomited for quite a long time since stopping the chemotherapy to have his radiotherapy.

It was a lovely day. Jack got to be a kid and play with all the other kids, and we helped him on the equipment. The play equipment was quite high, and it had many children on it from the party, so I was extra careful with Jack. I wanted him to have fun but not get in the way of all the other kids. We were sitting at the very top, and I was getting worried, the kids were really mucking around up there. The edge was so close.

I was trying to tell them to be careful of the edge, it was such a long way up. One of the dads saw that I was anxious and said, "Don't worry too much about them. If they fall, they will learn. They will only do it once!"

I really thought about what to say, and I had to answer him with, "You're right … they will only do it once. Just like a little boy we see at the hospital who has a shunt in his brain and is learning to walk again to prove it. He fell off a slide." I said it peacefully, not meaning to be mean or anything, but just to make him aware.

I'm not sure if he knew what to say, but he smiled and said, "Oh, Okay."

The rest of the day went on quite smoothly. Jack fell asleep on one of the fold-out chairs, he must have had an awesome time. It was wonderful to see him have fun with the other kids today, because he had missed out on so much.

On the final day of Jack's long radiotherapy haul of forty treatments, Luke and I decided to go into the hospital to meet all the people that Anthony and Jack had spoken so highly of each and every day. They all got a kick out of seeing Luke, all the nurses needed to have a hold of him. Jack showed me what he did every single day, how he would run down into the toy room and play, usually with a ball he loved from their toy box. Unfortunately, the ball had gone missing a few days before. He showed me the radiotherapy room and picked a sticker to go on the final number on his chart, it was now full.

They put him under the anaesthesia, and it was so hard to leave him there, although I knew this time would be only for a short period. The look of everything was so scary, his mask, the size of the machine compared to him. It was a difficult moment, I must say. I was proud of Anthony for doing this with Jack on his own.

After his final session of radiotherapy, we went back into the waiting room, where the group of doctors and nurses had presents for Jack. They had really thought about the gifts. It amazed me to think that in such a short period of time, they could know Jack so well.

Hanna was the girl who had taken a shine to Jack. She knew that every day he would come in and play with this one ball in the toy room, but towards the end the ball went missing, which disappointed Jack. He was so happy with the routine of it all. She bought him another special ball, which was really weird. It was red and covered in a mesh, so that when you squeezed it these green lumps would form on the ball, piercing through the mesh. When you let go, they would retract. Jack thought it was brilliant.

One of the anaesthetists gave Jack a teddy bear with a sling on his arm. When he gave it to Jack, he said, "Now Jack, when you are all better and feeling well, you can take the sling off of the teddy bear."

That was sweet. I looked forward to the day that Jack would be cured from this horrible disease. I knew it would be a very long time before I would be happy in taking that sling off of the bear, but I truly did look forward to when we could do it together.

So, radiotherapy was finally over. Jack's hair was looking lovely. He was looking great, and it seemed like he was getting back to his normal self. We knew that it would be short-lived, because Jack would have to start the next load of chemotherapy. Each cycle would go for eight weeks now instead of four weeks. He would have four rounds, making eight months all up. We would have to watch him suffer again and lose all that beautiful hair he had just grown.

Why can't it just be gone? Why can't they say to us, "Hey there's no more cancer, and we don't need to give Jack any more chemotherapy. He's been cured!"

Although in my head I did believe that could happen, I also realised that we lived in this human world, and a miracle like that could never happen in real life. Or could it?

"Where's my miracle?" I would ask. It's got to be coming some time now, surely.

CHAPTER 20

Sometimes things that happen in our lives cannot be explained. They are confusing. Although confusing to us it doesn't mean they are confusing to God. It doesn't mean that they are negative or should be judged. There is always a reason for everything that happens and even if we cannot see it now, there will come a time when our eyes will understand its value. All things happen for the greater good.

It was mid-March when Jack's chemotherapy started again, and so did all the other things that were on our list. Anthony had returned to work, but my network of help was always there. Jack had another hearing test, and this time, it was not as good of a result as I had hoped. The woman testing him told me that Jack's higher pitch of hearing was not working at all. This was one of the things that could happen with chemotherapy and radiotherapy, we knew that, but I was surprised that all of a sudden, he couldn't hear anything high-pitched, like smoke alarms.

I was there by myself in that room listening to a woman telling me that my son had lost some of his hearing. I was devastated. I knew that it was only one part, but it was a part of him. All I could imagine was Jack older and living alone somewhere and the smoke detector going off and him not being able to hear it.

It was something small that meant a great deal to me, because I felt like Jack just kept on having things that were a part of everyone else's normal life taken away. His walking, his coordination and ball skills, his ability to just play, his talking, his blinking, his smile, and now this, his hearing. How do you stop the need to just be sad and stay that way? It's so hard to continue down such a tiresome and negative road. Were these people, right?

I returned home feeling empty, but Jack was so happy. He was always happy, and that made me feel a little better, knowing that he was not letting this all get to him. He was still being a kid and having a good time as much as he could when he could. I told Anthony about the hearing test, and he felt the same as I did, a little tired of nothing going Jack's way.

We began Jack's chemotherapy rounds again, and it was nice to know that we were only going to be in the hospital overnight for two nights every two months now instead of every month. While Jack was lying in the hospital bed having his drugs put through him, something really strange happened. He started talking about an orange man. Nansie and I looked at each other and thought that he was maybe just mucking around, but no, Jack was looking at an orange man.

"What do you mean by orange?" I asked Jack.

"He's wearing orange all over," Jack said.

We started to ask him more questions about this orange man, like, "Where is he?"

"He's in the window!" Jack yelled as if it were a game. He pointed at the big hospital window from his bed, where he was playing with his cars.

We were five levels up and staring at the big beautiful blue sky with lovely white clouds dancing around it. Nansie and I once again looked at each other as Jack smiled at this man we could not see.

"What is the man doing?" I asked him.

"Nothing," Jack said. "He's just watching me play." Jack then looked down at his cars and continued to play.

"What shoes is he wearing, Jack?" Nansie asked him.

Jack raised his head to look up at the window to see the man. Then answered, "Big black boots." He put his head back down to play as if it were no bother to him.

Nansie said to me, "Maybe the drugs are causing hallucinations."

That actually made a lot of sense. I decided to go with that theory, but it did put my stomach in a knot whenever he would, here and there, announce the orange man's return.

I would randomly ask Jack, "Where's the orange man now?"

He would sometimes say, "He's gone."

I felt so much more at ease when the orange man wasn't hanging around watching Jack. But thinking hard about it, should I really be worried? Jack was happy when the orange man was there with him. Maybe it was an angel? An angel made me feel a little more at peace about it, until Nansie decided to inform me, "Don't people in prison wear orange outfits with black boots?"

Thanks, Nansie! Now I have an image of the orange man in my mind, and when Jack tells me he's returned, it will be a cellmate in orange overalls and black boots, maybe even with handcuffs on. Great! An angel I ask? I don't think so!

When we returned home from the hospital after Jack's first full treatment, the orange man came to live with us. Jack told us where he would stand, right at the corner of the hallway. I strangely found myself diverting around him as I walked up the hallway, even though there was nothing there. Or was there? He wasn't visiting us all the time, of course, only when Jack spotted him and yelled out, "The orange man is here!"

Please go away Mr. Orange Man! You're freaking me out.

One morning, I got up early with Jack. It was around five thirty. He was sitting on his knees in the kitchen, I was sitting on the floor in the toy room, and we were rolling a ball along the tiled floor to each other. We were trying to be really quiet; Anthony and Luke were asleep still, and all was silent and dark, with only the toy room light on. We kept rolling the ball back and forth to each other, having a great time, and then Jack just stopped. He was staring at the spot in the hallway where the orange man appeared to him.

"What's wrong, Jack?" I asked.

This broke his trance, and he shrugged his shoulders and answered me with, "Oh, it's just the orange man. He's here again."

I smiled at Jack, because by this time I had become used to the orange man being around. He never did anything; he just stood there in the corner of the hallway, so I felt quite comfortable.

I thought I would entertain Jack, so he believed that I believed he could see the orange man. I asked, "What's he doing now?"

I was expecting the same answer as he always gave, which was, "He's just watching me play." But instead, Jack said, "He's gone up into Luke's room to watch him."

My eyes opened wide and I said, "What? Luke's room?"

"Yeah," Jack replied,

"Why?" I asked

Jack said, "Just to watch him."

My whole body was frozen, and I mean frozen. I felt my heart beating out of my chest.

My mind started screaming at me, *Run to Luke now! Go and see if he's okay ... run!* but I couldn't move, not even a muscle.

I had never felt this way before in my life. I was frozen with fear! The time felt like forever. It was probably a good five minutes before I could even speak.

"What's wrong, Mummy?" Jack asked as he got off the floor and came into the toy room to play something else.

"Nothing," I whispered.

Slowly, muscle by muscle, I dragged myself up off of that floor and made my way to Luke's room, switching every light on in the house as I went. I made it there to find him ... sleeping peacefully. I don't know what I was expecting, maybe the rocking chair moving back and forth, but there was nothing, just the peaceful sound of Luke's breathing. I left his door open a little wider than usual.

We decided during this group of chemotherapy that we would go on a much-deserved holiday (no orange man invited) and accept an opportunity to go to the holiday house that belonged to the children's cancer charity group that had visited us initially in hospital. It was called the Samuel House named after a little boy, who was a twin, who had lost his battle with cancer some time ago. The parents donated the land and then raised funds to have the house built and decorated for families associated with the children's cancer charity.

I was expecting a shack that was rundown and old, but I was wrong. It was a lovely three-bedroom house with a kitchen and lounge and a beautiful games room that was later to be called "the big massive toy room" by Jack. It had a pinball machine, foosball, TV with a popular game console, heaps of books, puzzles, and games. We were all impressed.

There was a lovely balcony that looked over a backyard with some play equipment and an area shaded with a sail. The play equipment looked a little tired, but it was still a great place to go when Jack got bored.

We set up a play gym area for Luke inside, so he could see the television. We threw some toys in it that we found, and he loved it. It was quite a relaxing place to go, and with so many activities for the kids to get involved with, it was fun. We invited a few family members and friends up one day for a barbecue, which made it so much more enjoyable, sharing such a wonderful place with those who loved and supported us. We all had a great day full of fun, food, and games together, and everyone agreed what a special place this was.

My friend who the kids called Aunty Jenny brought her face-painting kit and had the endless job of painting the kids' faces, hands, arms, feet, and whatever they could get painted. Jack was a funny about getting his face painted, but Aunty Jenny painted him to look like Daddy, giving him a beard and a moustache. She then turned him into a pirate, and he even allowed a red-backed spider on his hand.

The children played on the play equipment. The slide seemed to be placed in the wrong position, as it was going down a downhill slope. When you got to the end, the hill was so steep that you just kept going. It was funny to see the bigger kids tackle the slide and sometimes end up on the ground. They loved it! But with Jack, we were much more cautious, making sure we always had a catcher at the bottom.

Samuel House was situated in a beautiful area, with each surrounding house owning a bit of land and a beautiful view. In the mornings, we would watch kangaroos hopping through the fields as we drank our coffee on the balcony. What a calming and beautiful place to be! We were so grateful to have this opportunity for a small piece of time away where we felt comfortable and rested, one that we could share with the people around us. We could not thank the connected children's cancer charity enough for this gift. After the few days we had there were over, and we had explored the small country town and its many playgrounds and sights, we returned back home ... to the real world.

Not long after our lovely holiday, Anthony and I took the boys to the shops one afternoon. While Anthony was putting Jack into the car in the shopping centre car park, a gentleman was looking at me strangely. He began to walk over towards me. He smiled and then apologised for acting a little strange.

"My name is Steve," he started. "I couldn't help but notice your son's scar on the back of his head. I'm sorry to pry, but it's just that my daughter has had head surgery, and she is fine now."

I looked at him inquisitively, as it seemed to be a weird coincidence that he had seen us.

"I am a supplier of a product through a company called V.M-Tech," he continued (I have changed the name of this company to a self-made name) "which I do because I believe that without it, my daughter would have not survived. Here's my card, and please ring me if you would like to know anything about it. You could also go on the website and read about it first if you like."

I took Steve's card and thanked him. He smiled and continued on his way.

The first thing that I did when I got home was to look on the internet about all the V.M-Tech products. There were a few, but the most important one was a potent vitamin powder. The information about it was quite in-depth yet easy to understand. It made a great deal of sense to me, and I considered the product a lot over the next few months.

I rang Steve and had a few talks to him, and he suggested using it while Jack was on the chemotherapy, as it would help his cells recoup and improve the immune system. I was thinking that the whole idea was to kill the bad cells and all other cells, and the thought that I might be hindering that made me not want to use it. Steve tried to explain to me several times that it would be nourishing the body so that it would be able to handle the chemotherapy and assisting the body in doing what it was meant to do, and that was kill the cancer.

For some reason, I had in the back of my mind that I didn't want to start this stuff until Jack was finished with his medicine. But after many, many months of going back and forth about it, I finally decided to give it a go. Ma has always encouraged me to try more natural ways, and she went with me to see Steve and I ordered my first lot of V.M-Tech products.

We were a good way through Jack's final eight months of chemotherapy and all had basically gone as it would normally go. I thought it would be a good time to start him with something natural to help in any way it possibly could. We tried the main parts to V.M-Tech, which also included these little gummy bears full of the special vitamin powder and many other good things.

It was really hard to get the stuff into Jack, because the tablets were humongous, and I had to crush them and mix them with water and then syringe them into his mouth. I made sure I tried everything to see what it tasted like, and it was horrid. The amounts that needed to be given to him were quite large, but we tried our best to get as much as we could into him, thinking that anything would be of benefit. The best thing I purchased were nourishing gummy bears, because they were yummy.

I had to definitely explore my natural options, because there had been many incidents throughout this experience that made me question our Western medicine. There were too many mistakes being made, or nearly being made if it weren't for Anthony and I questioning people's actions. During these final treatments, there was a moment when a doctor who I had never seen before told me that Jack would be having his chemotherapy soon. I looked at her strangely, because this particular day we were not having chemotherapy.

"Chemotherapy? You mean pentamidine?" I asked.

She looked at me confused, looked back down at her chart to reconfirm with herself. Then she said, "Yes, he is having his chemotherapy today called pentamidine."

I smiled at her as a hundred different questions went through my mind. *Am I wrong? Have I got this incorrect? No, I don't think so,* I thought, and so I answered with, "Yes, Jack will be having his pentamidine *only* today, which is, I thought, an antibiotic, not a chemotherapy drug!"

She looked at me and quickly brushed the whole incident off with a quick, "Yes, yes, yes, that's correct." The way she looked at me, I could tell she had absolutely no idea.

Really? I am supposed to trust you, I thought. *No wonder I trust no one!*

I used to be so trusting, always giving others the benefit of the doubt, but after so many times of the trust failing, you become automatically unable to trust anymore.

The doctors and nurses would get so many things wrong, which made me frustrated and annoyed. But there were times when their words of incompetence were like a breath of fresh air, and that is when they were proven wrong.

Jack, as you know, had a hearing test, and it was stated that he now had high-pitch deafness to things like smoke detectors. So, the day that I burnt the toast for breakfast and set the smoke alarm off was quite a wonderful day.

Jack was running out of the lounge with his hands over his ears screaming, "What's that noise? What's that noise?"

Anthony and I just looked at each other smiling and shaking our heads, knowing that once again they had gotten it wrong. That was a good feeling, I must say. It felt like we had won a small but significant battle that day. My son had not lost his hearing in any way.

Don't believe everything that everyone has to say, even those with certificates and years of knowledge. In my experience they didn't always know.

CHAPTER 21

Even in the hardest moments there are times when we can smile, have a laugh and find joy. Be the one that makes people laugh when all they want to do is cry. Bring happiness when others are consumed by sadness. Bring joy whenever the moment feels like joy will never be found again. This is the beginning to healing the pain.

We had planned a wonderful third birthday for Jack this year, and it was *Cars* themed, with the main character being Lightning McQueen! Jack was so excited about his birthday, probably because he knew that he would be ripping open a whole bunch of presents and eating Nansie's chocolate cake. We had decorated the family room in red and black and had set up a children's party table for all the kids who would attend.

Jack received two identical huge red Lightning McQueen cars as presents, one from Uncle Shane and his family and one from Sarah and her family. Sarah quickly took hers back and drove home, swapping one of the large red McQueen cars for exactly the same thing but in blue, just so that Jack would not have two of the same gift. How sweet! I don't think Jack would have cared at all. It was amazing that she even had another one at home to swap with.

Luke was such a great kid. He played mostly with the wrapping paper that was left on the carpet after Jack had been there. Luke never gave us any trouble. He was an easy-going baby and was happy to crawl around and check things out for himself. He was so cute that most of the time, someone just wanted to pick him up and cuddle him, which he hated ... *not!*

The only thing you couldn't do with Luke was take things away from him, especially food. When we were making a cake one day, I let Jack and Luke share the spoon to lick the batter from it. All of us couldn't stop laughing at the crazy child we had in Luke every time Jack tried to get the spoon back from him. We resorted to using two spoons after it was obvious Jack would no longer be getting his hands-on Luke's spoon.

At Jack's birthday, we played a few games like pass the parcel. It felt so good that Jack really enjoyed his birthday, because a year earlier he had not been well at all. It would be a week from now this time last year that all this illness had been discovered. What a year it had been!

So now we were coming to the end of Jack's treatment. In the overall scheme of things, that would mean that he would be cured and that from here on in it would all be about rehabilitation. Dr. Marlene had organised referral letters to different doctors concerning Jack's facial paralysis and his eyes. We weren't sure what our options would be, but it would definitely be good to have a chat with someone who was really knowledgeable in both of those areas.

When Jack's final overnight stay with chemotherapy was over, Jack came home to a massive present on his bed. It was from Nansie. He opened it, and it was two different massive garbage trucks. Wow! It also had this DVD called *Where Does the Garbage Go?* Jack watched it over and over again. Now he had his own garbage trucks to play with. Awesome!

We sat at the outside table as Jack filled the small bin with marbles that was attached to the garbage truck. He pressed the button on the truck that lifted the bin and emptied its contents into the truck, noises and all. The heavy smell of chemotherapy pouring from his body was always profound after the three full days in hospital. I remember thinking that I wouldn't have to smell this horrible smell on him ever again. We still had the vincristine and etoposide left to administer, but that never made him smell like this. I watched him happily play with his new trucks and couldn't wait until the end of his treatment.

The day finally came. The very last day of Jack's treatment forever. I was so happy and excited, and I had Nansie right by my side. I think it was the fact that we would no longer be so connected to this hospital. We would be free. I remember sitting on one of the recliners with Jack asleep on me while he was having the last vincristine. I was feeling almost ecstatic ... until Samantha, our social worker, came up to me and started talking.

"So, this is the last treatment for Jack!" she said. I nodded as she continued, "How do you feel about that?"

I blurted out, "I can't wait till it's over and we never have to do this again!"

"Oh, that's good!" she said. "Are you worried about not having any more treatment, or are you content with that?"

"I'm so happy about that!" I answered her. "I can't wait to be free of this place."

Samantha smiled, patted my shoulder and said, "Good for you," and left.

Then I had time to process that conversation for the next hour and realised why she had been concerned about me. There was the possibility that all would not be well with Jack and the treatment would fail. Once the cell-killer, chemotherapy, was no longer going through Jack's body, would the cancer grow back? Maybe that thought had always been at the very back of my subconscious mind, but today I had been so happy for that one moment, knowing that this stupid way of treating cancer would never have to be in our routine ever again.

Maybe I felt that I would finally be free to also try more natural ways with Jack. Now that we had done our time, we could move on with our lives and help Jack to finally rehabilitate towards being that normal, healthy child we once knew. But now there was this added weight on my shoulders, the idea that the cancer could come raging back. If it did, there really wouldn't be many options for Jack.

I had to stay in the moment. That was how I had lasted this long, wasn't it? By allowing myself to live a day at a time. What I didn't like was that now, in the depths of my soul, there was the voice of *what if*. I stayed positive and believed that Jack would be healed, but did I believe without an ounce of doubt? I don't think I did. I tried to keep my mind at ease, and I was truly excited when we walked out of the hospital that day. I felt like the chains had been unlocked, and we were finally free of their western medical ways.

Perhaps I have been a little bit judgmental throughout this book towards the hospital. In fact, there were many beautiful people who crossed our paths during that time, and most of them were there to help people and save lives. I thank them all for doing such a wonderful job. It could not be an easy job, but one of pure heartache to watch these beautiful children suffer. Many of these medical professionals truly believed that this was the best way to a cure.

My eyes have been opened wide now, and I realised that we are not in control...not here. If others believe their way is right, they can take over your beliefs as a parent and make you do it anyway. That day, I felt like I was free of an institution that really didn't know the answer but instead used the best options they had. I appreciate all they did for my son, and I thank them and wish they had convinced me that they honestly had the answer I was looking for.

In my mind, all I said was, *we are not coming back!*

Yes, I knew I had to come back for MRIs, pentamidine, and check-ups, but it was different now, and so I repeated to myself:

We are not coming back! Not like this again.

CHAPTER 22

Winning means never giving up, no matter the odds. You truly come to believe that even when you have lost, you can still win. You can see beyond the minor foes and tests in your life and identify the truth. The ultimate and final result is determined by your determination. Live for the moment so that the knowledge you obtain is positive and true. Embrace it and use it for the rest of your time.

W e had spent six to eight weeks having the best time ever. We could do whatever we wanted without the thought of having to go to the hospital for chemotherapy or drugs of any kind. We went shopping, and we always took Jack's little wallet that was full of gold coins. Every time we passed a children's ride, we had to stop, because Jack wanted to have a ride on it...and we let him!

Yes, it did cost a lot every time we went out, but boy, it was worth it to watch him be so happy. We would also buy him a dinosaur donut from the donut shop for morning tea. We had a great time. Jack's hair was starting to grow back, and he was looking like a healthy young boy again.

The day arrived for Jack's after-treatment MRI, it was early December. We had scheduled one previously, but because of complications and the doctors running behind like last time, I chose to go home and wait no longer. It was easier for us to go home and give Jack food and drink and come back another day than to hang around not knowing what time he would eventually go in. This occurred a couple of times throughout the course of his treatment, and I think they knew me well enough now and what I would prefer to do. It was just too hard to ask Jack to not eat for a period of eight hours or more. No one should have to, especially a child.

On this day, Jack, Ma, and I were back, and things were running smoothly so far. I was so nervous about this MRI. Afraid might be a more appropriate word because this would indicate whether Jack had a good chance of being cancer-free from now on. All the other MRIs had shown no signs of any cancer, but this one was different. This one followed six to eight weeks of no treatment at all, nothing to exterminate the evil disease that once was inside of him.

It was getting close to the time when Jack would go in. We had completed all the necessary documentation and his port had been assessed ready for him to have his anaesthetic medication put through it. Then through the door walked in Dr. Marlene. I was surprised to see her, because she had never come into this section before to see us.

My happy hello was taken away when I thought, *Why is she here? What's wrong?*

"Can we talk somewhere private for a minute?" she asked me.

I looked her in the eyes and said, "Oh no, what?"

"Oh gosh, I'm not the Grim Reaper or anything! Don't worry," she said. "There is just something important I need to address with you."

We went into a private room where Jack sat on my lap and Ma waited outside. My palms were sweating, I was sick to my stomach, and I couldn't breathe properly.

"Now, there has been a situation uncovered within our pharmacy department that I need to inform you of," she began.

"Oh?" I answered.

"It's been found that through human and computer error, some children, eleven in total, have been overdosed with their etoposide phosphate medication. It has been completely investigated and determined that the extra dosages given would not cause any damage, in the amounts that were given. The programme on the computer was automatically working out the correct dosages and then the operators thought that they also had to do it manually, which caused these children's etoposide PH amounts to be more than what they were supposed to have."

What?

I just looked at her while she tried to explain the scientific way they worked out the dosages and how they actually were being worked out. Someone new had entered this role and uncovered the mistakes that were being made. I didn't care about that. She had assured me that the amounts given were still in the safe range and that all would be fine. She was very confident because Jack had missed some of his etoposide medication throughout his chemotherapy when his blood levels were too low. I was coping with all of this information, I think. Then she had to tell me that there could possibly be side effects.

"What side effects?" I asked.

Can you guess the side effects before I tell you what she said? Yes, the side effects were ... wait for it! ... hmm, maybe leukaemia or his cancer returning in his brain or even somewhere else in his body. I couldn't help the tears; she gave me a tissue, but this was just too much. Too much!

What else can you people do to Jack, to us? What else? Did I walk him into a place that was going to kill him instead of saving him?

Jack wanted to see Ma, so I opened the door and let him go to her. She could see through the doorway that I had been crying. I sat back down, and to be honest, I can't remember a lot more after that except the last thing she said to me.

"I am organising a letter for each family to explain what happened, and every family affected by this has been or is being personally contacted. People on the outside who have not been affected by this are not going to understand it completely, and they could get the wrong information. We don't want this. They might think it has been all kids or more kids, but it was definitely just eleven. It would be appreciated if we could keep this information to only the ones who are affected. We don't want a huge panic happening because of this situation, we don't want lots of people contacting us wondering if it was them or not them. So, we don't want it getting out."

I looked at her. She was staring at me like she was waiting for an answer.

"Fine," I said.

She continued to look at me, and then she said, "So what should we do about Grandma then?"

I was completely confused. *What on earth did Ma have to do with it?* I thought.

"What do you mean?" I asked with a blank look on my face.

"What... should we do... about Grandma?" she asked me again, but this time she said it a bit slower and more pronounced. Then my brain kicked in and I think I went into shock.

"Grandma? No, she's fine, no worries, no, she'll be fine," I mumbled. She appeared happy with my blubbering answer. She apologised for this incompetency and left.

I sat there in that lonely room thinking and thinking about what had just happened. The truth was that the hospital didn't want anyone talking to the media and leaking it. She didn't want me talking to good old Grandma in case Grandma told someone. I began to boil! I realised the whole of what had just happened.

How dare you! I thought.

I was so angry. I walked out of that room and rang Anthony straight away. "You have to come here right now, and I mean right now!" I quickly explained to him what I could, and then Jack was called to go in for his MRI. I did not tell Ma what happened, but Anthony did.

I know people who I could tell this to! I could make this huge! It may even give me some sense of pleasure, but for what? I had better things to care about than that!

My thoughts were more worried about the fact that this had gone on for a long time and that it took a new employee to realise a mistake that never should have happened ... never! They poisoned my child by using the drug that should be curing him, to the point where it could kill him. Oh, it shouldn't cause him any harm, but it could! What a load of bullshit!

I had never known such incompetency in all my life. It was a joke to me, an unbelievable joke! I just couldn't understand why this was happening to Jack. It was like a magnet of hurt and pain and unending wrongs. The more positive I tried to be, the worse it got.

It had been one of the hardest days we had to endure for a long time, and yet every day was hard. It just puts into perspective how much extra pain and cruelty had been caused that was not necessary in this horrific trial of ours. From just the small things like being made to wait for so long every day to this. The amount of suffering caused by this place had been more than we could bear. They were supposed to be helping Jack and helping us. Instead they were like a disease themselves.

We returned home, and we were exhausted. There wasn't any other way to describe it. We now had this challenge of trying to deal with the fact that Jack might get sick again.

That night, we got Jack and Luke off to sleep finally, and then my mobile phone rang. It was Dr. Marlene. I was unsure of why she was ringing us, but after the day we had, I was sure it was to just confirm all the things she had already been through with us, maybe another apology ... but it wasn't.

"I'm sorry to ring you so late," she began, "but I have the results from Jack's MRI, and I'm sorry to say that they are not good."

"What?" *I can't believe it. This is not real.*

"It is actually showing that the cancer has returned. It is now in his brain and spinal fluids and has become quite aggressive."

NO! NO!

I'm not sure how I was sounding or if I was actually saying anything at all. She asked me to pass the phone over to Anthony, and so I did. I ran to the kitchen to get a glass of water, but I found that my body was just unable to cope with the small task. My hands were shaking, and it was so hard to breathe. I dropped the glass into the sink and went down the hallway looking up to the ceiling and screaming, "You're not taking him! You're not taking him! I won't allow it!"

I went to my bedroom where I grabbed the home telephone, and somehow, I rang Nansie. I was on the floor sobbing, "It's back! It's back!"

When Nansie answered the phone, she had no idea what was going on. She even had to ask who it was.

"It's back, Mum!" I screamed.

"What's back?" she asked.

"Jack ... the cancer is back!"

"I'm coming over," she said as she hung up the phone.

I lay there on the floor unable to do anything but rock myself with my face in my hands, sobbing.

This cannot be happening! How can we deserve this pain! I just don't understand what we have done that was so wrong. I don't understand.

I got up and went into Jack's room and just watched him, his beautiful face, such a beautiful kid. How could I live without him? I can't ... I can't live without him! I won't!

Anthony had finished the conversation with Dr. Marlene and he told me what she had said, that the cancer was back, and Jack now had metastasis of the brain. One small cancerous cell had hidden away and made it through all the treatment. Now that Jack's immune system had been destroyed by the chemotherapy, the cancerous cell or cells were able to run wild through his body within the spinal and brain fluids. He had no defence system; we had killed it, hoping that it would kill the cancer too.

That was the theory, anyway. The cancerous cells were more likely to die first before the good cells. Now we had nothing. No chance, nothing to try to save our wonderful little boy. How could I do nothing?

Stuff you, God, oh great one. Stuff you! So full of miracles and wonder. We are so in awe of you. For what? This was your chance to prove yourself to us, to everyone. Are you even really there? I just don't know anymore.

Nansie came over, but there wasn't anything to say. We just relayed what Dr. Marlene had said. Nansie was tough, when she needed to be. Anthony had the job of phoning Ma and Pa and letting them know. It was like a second blow to us all.

CHAPTER 23

Let's build each other up, instead of breaking each other down. We exist to make other people's lives better. To bring comfort to those who suffer. To bring joy to those who weep. To give food to those who hunger. The duty of every human being is to be of service to the rest of humanity. There is always something that you can give, there is always someone who is worse off than you.

We had arranged an appointment with Dr. Marlene to have a private conversation about Jack's results and to look at the MRI with her in a couple of days. Both mothers agreed to watch the boys while we went to the appointment. There was no need for them to attend such a morbid meeting. That dreaded day came, and as we walked from the car to the hospital, Anthony and I held hands tightly.

I turned and said to him, "No matter what happens today, I want you to know how much I love you and that nothing could ever change that."

He pulled me close to him as we walked and quickly responded, "Me too. I love you so much."

We got to the chemotherapy area, and we sat in that horrible waiting room again. Nurses who knew us that walked past would say hello.

All I thought was, *Do they know? Are they wondering why we are here by ourselves?*

Without fail, in the state that we were in, with no one else waiting in that room, we sat there and waited ... and waited ... and waited. Twenty minutes passed, and I just shook my head. Really? In all our pain, we were still made to wait.

My son is dying and instead of being with him I am sitting in this horrible waiting room, my valuable time being wasted away!

Finally, Dr. Marlene came in and hugged us and showed us to a room where we could talk. She pulled out the scans and apologised for the terrible day that had unfolded; with the news of the overdose and Jack's relapse all at once. Why was she sorry? It wasn't her fault, but she was the representative of a hospital that in my eyes had made many mistakes. Too many.

She switched on the light for the X-rays to be shown on the X-ray box on the wall, but the light didn't turn on.

"Sorry, this one is a bit dodgy!" she said as she gave it a whack and it fluttered a little. Dr. Marlene gave it another huge slap with her hand, and the light shot on. "That's how you make things work around here!"

We had a small giggle, but deep down I was shocked. How can you take a place seriously when you have to do something like that just so your equipment will work?

What else works like this? Is this the standard with everything around here? You have over-dosed my son and now you are about to show me his killer! What have I done? Leaving him in your hands.

It made me feel like they had been a part of all this not working for Jack. I knew they had done all they could, but Jack was my son, and their best wasn't good enough. The picture flashed on, and the doctor showed us how the cancer had metastasised now in the original spot and spread itself out on a massive scale. It had started to thicken Jack's spinal fluids. It was everywhere! How could this be? It had only been a matter of weeks!

Who is to blame? Had we all done this to him?

We had killed off his only life support, his immune system, and now it seemed we were all to blame for this. Why didn't we try another option? I knew that if I didn't try every avenue, I could not live with myself. I tried their way. I did everything they told me to do. Everything they had forced me to do. I suffered as Jack had suffered through their long exhausting and complicated methods, and now here I was staring at an outcome that did not leave us any choices.

I looked long and hard at the image of Jack's small head. I looked at every little bit of the disease that had started taking him over. Then I realised that I was looking right at the devil. Eye to eye, we were staring at each other.

So, you have the upper hand with us, but you will never win! Never!

This was what it meant to have the devil roaming our world. There he was, standing right in front of me. Eating away at Jack's innocent life.

We discussed our options with Dr. Marlene, which really there were none. More chemotherapy might, in his current state, not be of any benefit at all, and he would be vomiting with it. We agreed that we weren't going to do that to him, and then we asked how long he had left. She told us that he would have up to twelve weeks.

Twelve weeks! I only have twelve weeks left with my Jack!

We chose to keep Jack home and stay with him there unless any reason came up that he needed to be brought in to the hospital. One minute we were celebrating the end of his treatment, a moment that for me was bittersweet. I had always been afraid of this day, but I didn't believe it would stomp on me so quickly after.

There wasn't much left for us to say, but apparently there was a lot more that had to be said. A lady from the palliative care department came knocking on the door so that she could let us know they would be completely supporting us through Jack's final days. They didn't go into a full description of what would be happening but just grazed over the points of some drugs that he may soon need when his condition worsened.

There was another tap at the door, and there was Samantha, our social worker.

"You wanted to see me, Dr. Marlene?"

"Yes, come in, Samantha. Did you get my email?"

"No." Samantha paused as she looked around the room a little bewildered. "What's happening?" She came in and sat down by the door. Once again, we heard Dr. Marlene explain, to Samantha this time, Jack's circumstances. It brought me to tears yet again.

"I'm so sorry!" said Samantha.

Anthony was angry, I could tell. It was all so unorganised.

Did you get my email? Bloody ring her, for heaven's sake. Talk, people! This is my son, mine! He is not just a number or some statistic. How are we supposed to react to that?

The last time I'd seen Samantha, it was the last day of Jack's treatment. The way Dr. Marlene had told us about Jack and then Samantha, it felt like she had done it millions of times before. Just another day at work.

How many times have you done this? I thought. *How many times? I know that this can't be easy for you, but can't you just make sure that it's as easy as it possibly can be for us? It wasn't. They were making us suffer even more.*

Once again, I felt as though we had been tormented. It took every ounce of strength I had inside to keep from just getting up and leaving, but then that would give them something to use against me.

Maybe she needs counselling? Obviously, she's angry and upset. Maybe she needs more support? Maybe she needs help? Maybe ... Maybe ... Maybe ... then I wouldn't hear the last of it. They would be pushing their ways that just don't work on us once again. Now it's my turn, my turn to try something else. I refuse to let you tell me that Jack's life is over. I will never give up on him! Never!

"Ring us when you need us or if you have any questions," Dr. Marlene said, and then we left and drove home.

When we arrived, the boys were asleep. We discussed with our mothers what we had been told. Nansie said no to any more drugs; let his hair grow back and let him have a great time for as long as he possibly can. That meant nothing but love and a whole bunch of fun.

Ma was quite the opposite. She wanted us to try different things naturally. I had books that I had been reading of huge success stories with people who had been completely full of cancer and survived without a trace in them in the end.

It's hard to explain to you how I was feeling; it was like I needed to be alone. I just went and laid across the bed thinking, *What can I do?* I was so sad. I felt guilty that I wasn't with Jack, holding him and kissing him, but for some strange reason I just wanted to be alone.

I rang some of my friends to tell them what had happened. Nansie rang my brother Shane, and the afternoon ended up with lots of family and friends being around us. I rang Aunty Jenny, who I leaned on because I felt like I could. She was someone I knew could just drop everything at any time if I needed her. She was at work, and I knew that it wasn't the best time to ring her, but I just had to talk it all through and get some ideas on where to go from here. The conversation went as best as it could, with us both just losing it.

She said, "That's it. I am coming right away!"

I felt selfish, because I knew that her boss wouldn't be happy with her. Only her and her sister actually worked there, but I knew that she would come not just for me but to see Jack and give him a cuddle.

I kept reading a cancer book on natural healing that I had been given, and there were contact phone numbers in it if you needed to order any products or talk to someone. I kept popping outside after more phone calls to different people and found Jack, Anthony, Poppie, and Uncle Shane playing cricket. Jack was having a great time, which was so good to see. He looked so good, so well. It was unbearable to think about how sick he really was.

Was this what it was going to be like, just as Nansie had said, give him a beautiful and wonderful time in his final days with us? I couldn't accept it, and I wouldn't.

There was so much information in the book about juicing and all these other products or natural foods that clean the body of all its toxins. I had to try something else. If people had been saved through eating pawpaw and only pawpaw, then that was what I would try.

Aunty Jenny arrived, which was hard. We were both just blubbering messes, confused and disoriented not knowing why or how this could have happened. I'd never really thought about not having Jack around. It's always in the back of your head, but you can never give any recognition that it is going to happen. Even now, I couldn't see my life without him. It was incomprehensible to me. So, in a good way, it made me feel like it was not meant to happen and that it was up to me to do something about it. The choices were mine now, and I had to answer to nobody because everybody else's wonderful theories had failed. It was my turn to try.

I discussed what I had read and finally, with everyone's agreement, rang the number in the book and eventually spoke to a woman named Amanda, who was in our state. She was very convincing, telling me that I should not listen to those doctors but instead know that Jack would be fine. We made an appointment in the next few days for her to come out and see us. It made me feel so much better, although I didn't really know what she was going to do to help us.

Ma gave us her juicer so that I could start trying to give Jack fresh fruit juices with ingredients like beetroot, carrot and also fruit ones with pawpaw in it. Apparently, these were the most important fruits and vegetables to drink. The problem was that you were supposed to buy a very, very expensive juicer. This juicer was more efficient at keeping all the nutrients within the drink, but we could not afford over a thousand dollars for it. I chose to use the one we were given instead. It was expensive, but nowhere near as expensive as that one was.

Amanda came and discussed a natural diet for Jack and a couple of products she would order for us that had been good in the fight against cancer. One was called Erase, it was supposed to kill bad bugs within the intestines that can cause many different illnesses. Jack had to take it a couple of times a day, and it was disgusting. Another was liquid pawpaw and also bovine cartilage.

She got me to read some inserts from a pamphlet that explained how good these products were at fighting cancer in the body. She would get them to me as soon as she had them, but in the meantime, we should start Jack on a healthy diet of just fruits and veggies. This was going to be hard to do with Jack because he loved food and his milk. A small amount of anything was fine, but we had to try to cut out all chocolates and sugars, which were the number-one feeders of cancer. All cereals and grains were a big no-no also.

I knew it would be difficult for Jack, so I kept it basic: natural substances for everything and loads of fruits and veggies. I tried so many different ways to get him interested in these foods, like making funny faces with them on the plate. The natural liquids like the pawpaw and bovine cartilage were sometimes too much for him to take. We still had medication that Jack needed to have that the hospital had given us.

The idea was to never give him anything with an ingredient you could not pronounce; it was all to be as natural as possible. I even went to giving him grapes dipped in carob, which became his big thing. I hate carob, but Jack did not seem to notice the difference. Phew!

I changed all my products around the house to more natural options (to the best of my knowledge) so that his body didn't have to deal with any other foreign chemicals. All I wanted his body to do was heal itself. It was hard at first, but it got easier. The hardest thing was buying fresh food every day, the natural products like the bovine cartilage were a hundred dollars a bottle. It was financially difficult to maintain the lifestyle, but I was determined to do it.

Amanda brought Jack a teddy bear, which he proceeded to tie heaps and heaps of ribbons around. We named him Bo because of all the bows Jack had tied. Amanda was so nice and genuine, but I felt like there must be more to do for him.

Can the answer only be getting the body to function correctly? There has to be more I can do.

· I continued to look on the Internet, and I found some books by a Dr. Hulda Clark, including *The Cure for All Cancers*. She had her own website, and it did concern me that the Erase product we had been using might be a take-off of this woman's product called Triplex. Two different companies selling the same product, but Dr. Hulda Clark was the one who had studied the effects of bugs in our intestines and had created it.

There was also a machine called a Zapper. Yes, it was called a Zapper! It was a square black pad strapped on each wrist that would send a gentle current through the body. This was to be done once or twice a day for a cycle of around forty minutes. Each pad had a blue and a red wire running from it that connected to a small box you would turn on. Ma really wanted to look into the Zapper. She ended up purchasing it and also the Triplex formula for us, which we started using as soon as it was sent to her. Ma had a great conversation with one of the ladies over the phone, explaining that Jack was just a child, and they agreed that these products would be fine for any age group, even the Zapper.

Jack was unenthusiastic towards the Zapper at first because it would get in the way of him playing. Once he got used to wearing it, it no longer bothered him. He was really an adaptable child; he just worked around everything that was put in front of him, and he continued on. All he wanted to do was to have fun, and we always tried to make it so that he could, to the best of his ability.

I had started a daily diary of medications, so I could keep up with all the products, both Western and natural, that I was giving him each day. It was also a good indicator of how Jack was progressing, as we wrote down in red any vomiting or weird moments we experienced with him.

When Dr. Marlene told us about Jack, we were asked if there was anything special we would like to do with him. Things like going to another state and swimming with the dolphins or having a final family holiday before he became really ill. The thought of Jack becoming ill in another state really scared us. I wasn't sure how we would cope if something were to happen while we were away.

We decided that we would return to Samuel House for a much-deserved break. Jack really loved the "big massive toy room," as he put it. That would be something very special that we could all do as a family and for Jack. He could walk along the beach and play at all the different playgrounds they had down there. We started to plan for the trip.

Meanwhile, we had a few visits from Amanda, which was great, but I still felt like there was more I could do. We were trying our best to take away all household chemicals and stick to natural foods, but most of the foods out there were not very natural at all. Buying natural every day was hard on the wallet because Jack ate and ate and ate all day. There were some products from the natural section I would buy just to keep him happy, like a few chips, spaghetti, and carob products like buckwheat and carob biscuits and rice cakes covered in carob. They were not the best-tasting things, but Jack saw them as treats. I do not know how he didn't realise that it wasn't really chocolate.

We continued to do our juices every day as well, which he loved, but the cost was starting to be a problem. Buying food every single day was difficult, but we just kept plodding along slowly, day by day.

We had been invited to the children's cancer charity's Christmas picnic. We were not sure about going, as there was so much happening right now. It did seem like a great idea for Jack to go and experience a few things that he hadn't done before, so we finally agreed to go. We left Luke at Ma and Pa's house, so we could concentrate on Jack. We arrived and saw so many things on this great big oval.

Jack was amazed and keen to go off and explore, but we had arrived a little late, and the kids in Jack's age group had already received their presents from Santa. Kym, the lovely girl who had organised these events through the charity, saw us and snuck us through the line, as they had Jack's present put aside for him. Jack went up onto Santa's knee and graciously accepted the gift, had his photo taken, and then went on his way.

Kym had heard the news about Jack and spoke to us holding back tears. What a hard job it was for her and all those who worked for the charity. Many parents had gladly volunteered their time, but I never could; it would just be too hard to watch so many children suffering. Jack ripped open the present, and it was a big Play-Doh kit with a dog in it. Man, Jack loved Play-Doh! He thought it was awesome.

We moved on because there were so many wonderful things to do, see, and play. There was a giant basketball hoop with a big blow-up ball and other giant games, like Snakes and Ladders and Connect Four. Jack loved kicking the giant blow-up dice around. We painted a clay dinosaur on a stick and a glittered star to hang on the Christmas tree. We had photos with two footballers from our favourite football team, Anthony had to be in the photo too, of course.

They also had real snakes. These were big, long, and fat, and Jack wanted to kneel down next to one and pat it as it slithered along the ground. He had no fear. Jack went into a farmyard area where a small parrot sat on his hand and then started to flap its wings. Jack got a little scared and naturally tried shaking the bird off his hand, but the parrot kept flapping. Finally, Jack flicked the bird off like a bug and moved away from it. He looked at us a little unsure, but Anthony and I both started laughing because it looked really funny. Jack started to laugh too.

It was time to get a ride on one of the many Harley Davidson motorbikes that were there being ridden by a club that had kindly donated their time for the day. Anthony and Jack went on one together with the driver. It was fantastic watching them cruise around the oval. It turned out to be a lovely day, and it made me feel like Jack had accomplished a lot.

CHAPTER 24

Leave your mark. You are here for such a short moment in history, make it count. Be the memory that has future generations talking. Be the role model that people change their ways to copy. Be the person who will teach the world respect for all. One person, one life, one chance to shine your light on the world to make it a better place. Be breathtaking!

My uncle Colin came over to the house to see us and told us that he and my aunty wanted to do something special for Jack the following Sunday. They wanted to have a big barbecue. Colin was going to get a police car and motorbike for Jack and the kids to sit on, but also, he was going to organise a fire engine to arrive as well. It sounded fantastic!

Colin had been on the police force his entire adult life, and he had slowly made his way up the ladder and accomplished so many great things. He was always studying, and at the moment he was helping to complete a wonderful book about the force. I agreed because it sounded wonderful, and I knew how much Jack would love to see the fire engine.

We had a chat about the past few weeks, and I was so unbelievably angry and sad.

I blurted out to him, "I just can't understand how we are unable to cure a disease that is so simple. Our bodies kill cancer every day; that's how it works. A single cell becomes abnormal from lack of oxygen and becomes a rogue cell that is then eaten up by the good cells, but for some reason in some people their bodies are not functioning correctly. It always comes down to the immune system in everything I have read, so why are we killing these cells good and bad? We are killing the very cells that are meant to help cure us! We are using chemotherapy, and yet it's just a Band-Aid for a little while, and when it's stopped the disease is able to run wild. There are absolutely no good cells left to fight, and bad cells have the ability to multiply twice as fast as good ones. We are not curing the reason why? Why did it happen in that particular person in the first place? We can kill all the cancer cells, yippee! But are we going to get cancer coming back? Of course, we are, because there is that reason, that unanswered question inside those bodies. Why did it start in the first place? Something is wrong, so why don't we fix that?"

Colin looked at me and said, "The way you just said that, you need to be doing something with that passion."

I just shook my head. Was I going to become a doctor and learn how to cure diseases? I don't think so. But the idea had crossed my mind many times. Although I was thirty-three years old, I'm sure I could do it!

I had read many things that might or might not be true, I had started to investigate everything I could about cancer. I read that fish oil was not the most wonderful omega for your body, quite the opposite in fact. Flaxseed oil was the oil the body actually needed for all omega-3 requirements. It even kept your skin elastic and younger looking.

Well, hell, baby, give me some of that!

There was some great information I had read about, the devastation within the body just through being in contact with one single bad chemical, one that could be found on the outside of some fruits. That is just one chemical out of all the chemicals our bodies take in every day. Chemicals through the air, food, and all our cleaning and body products. It's just amazing how our bodies can even cope. It amazed me we were not all dying from this disease!

One morning, I arose at two o'clock to feed little Luke, and I was watching an American news talk show that was on. The item being discussed was plastic baby bottles and the microwave. Now, I had stopped using our microwave because of the things Amanda had told me and the things I had read, but I did not know that these plastic bottles I had used for Jack and Luke were leaching a deadly chemical known as BPA into them. I was devastated! The next day, although it was a struggle, I found myself some glass baby bottles and never used the plastic ones again.

It was things like this that made me wonder, *Was this one of the reasons this happened to Jack?*

I questioned vaccinations too. How scary are those things? Actually, getting off your butt and reading about it could scare someone to death. It had been a sore point for me, and it was something I tried to tread carefully with. Although Jack had all his vaccinations and Luke had all except the first one, I had to study them all first.

Luke did not have the initial Hep B vaccination in hospital when he was born. After some conversations and research, I realised that it wasn't necessary, for my own reasons and because of what was said to me by my own doctors.

There is a chemical called thimerosal (also known as thiomersal) that is mercury and is linked with autism and neurological disorders. Australia has made its children's vaccinations thimerosal-free and had now for a little while. Researching these injections gave me that question again of why.

Is this why Jack got sick?

I realise that Jack could have been sick from anything, for it was only now that I really knew what was going on with him and his body. Oh, how

I wish I knew exactly what I know now back then. I think many things would have been different. I understand the disease a little bit better, and I would have really concentrated on natural alternatives with foods and other household products. I can look at so many different reasons why this happened to Jack, and it could have been a combination of multiple things that contributed to his cancer.

Sadly, I will never know exactly why Jack's body was not well enough to fight his cancer or why he initially had it start up in the first place. All I know is that it was something, whether one thing or many. The answer will never be revealed to me no matter how much I researched...but I still researched.

The immune system and the body's defence system could be the major keys here. The depletion of our oxygen in the sky, chemicals, just the way we live. Although the human race is wonderful at adaptation, how can we adapt to a place that is depleting every single thing we need to actually function well and survive? If all our bodies are doing is trying to clean and fix ourselves, how is there time to just be?

Sometimes I amazed myself with the things I would think up. My uncle was right: there was something I should do, but I never knew what. My whole life I had been afraid of life and the horrible things it could bring, such as rejection. If I ever tried anything and failed, then I was a failure and I quit. If anyone ever said something bad about me or targeted me for any reason, I believed them. I believed that I wasn't worth it. Maybe I was just preparing myself for this moment.

Ever since I was young, I had this feeling inside of me. It was probably inside of everyone, but I felt as if there was something I hadn't done yet, something bigger than all of this. I wished that I knew, and I hoped that all this effort was going to save Jack's life and prove to the world that miracles could happen. I wanted to change the world, the terrible things that happen, but I never realised that I could.

We agreed to have this wonderful barbecue at my uncle and aunty's house the following Sunday, which was the day after Nansie's sixtieth birthday, December 14. I was very stubborn about the whole healthy concept. I was really concentrating on Jack not consuming too much sugar. It was Nansie's Birthday. I knew what Nansie's chocolate cakes were like: a complete sugar rush.

"You have to let him have some cake! If everyone is having some, he will want some!" she said, but I refused.

A piece of cake was not important to me at all. Getting Jack well was the most important thing, so I made sure that Jack had enough carob grapes and strawberries to think that he was having chocolate.

I know that this sounds silly, but even though carob contains many different sugars like sucrose, fructose, and glucose they are sugars that the body does need differently, as I saw with the V.M-Tech products we were trying to give him. They were all looking at how the body needs different sugars, not just the one we pound into our bodies through junk foods. Refined sugar was the sugar we needed to stay clear of, and the carob chocolate did not contain caffeine like normal chocolate did.

So Nansie came up with a really great idea. For the first time ever in the history of time, she did not make a chocolate cake for her birthday. Instead she brought over this amazingly well-crafted watermelon fruit cake with candles. It was a big wedge of watermelon with toothpicks of fruit stuck into it with candles. It was all fruit and it was amazing!

We had presents and a sing-along with the cutting of the cake, and the kids were all happy. It was the adults who were disappointed about not having the chocolate cake. You can't please everybody!

CHAPTER 25

Random acts of kindness can be selfish, and that's great!
Giving to others will make you feel good, it will give you that
warm and fuzzy feeling inside. Giving can bring so much
happiness to others but the greatest happiness is your own.

The next day was the barbecue at Uncle Colin's house. I was excited to see what he had planned for the day. It was sure to be a big day. We had even organised to go and get professional photos done afterwards of the family. I just hoped that Jack and Luke would be able to last out this big day.

On the way, I realised that we had forgotten the kids' jackets, which was just so silly because it was quite cool. Anthony had to head back for them after he had dropped us off, which I felt bad about. My aunty showed

Jack her pet turtle, which he was intrigued by. He patted its hard shell and watched as it slowly moved along the floorboards of the loungeroom.

A police motorbike turned up, so we ran out to see it. There was also a police car. The policewoman gave Jack a police shirt and tie, and then she let us sit in the police car and sound the siren, which was cool.

Lots of our friends and family were starting to arrive. Their kids were amazed at the flashing lights and sirens. It was time to sit on the police motorcycle, and so I sat on it with Jack in front of me, and then I grabbed Luke as well while Nansie took photos. The boys were amazed at the vehicles.

It started to drizzle, so Uncle Colin grabbed an umbrella and lifted it over us, so we wouldn't get wet on the bike. Anthony turned up with the jackets, thank goodness. That was the most important thing, to get the kiddies warm.

Everyone was standing out the front of the house when all of a sudden, the fire truck pulled up with its sirens sounding and lights flashing. Wow! The kids just stood there with their mouths open. It was fantastic. Four firemen stepped out of the truck and came towards Jack, bearing gifts for him. One had a plush fireman dog that he gave to Jack, and there was this massive present wrapped up. Jack's eyes lit up because we all know how much he loved presents, and this one was mega huge. He ripped it open, and there was the biggest toy fire truck I had ever seen. Thank goodness I had my sunglasses on, because my eyes were full of tears.

It was time to investigate the real fire truck and have a go at the fire hose. All the kids and some of the adults, Aunty Jenny included, had a go at squirting the big hose. Jack had a go, and he didn't want to stop. He was having a wonderful time. We all were.

There was one more thing, and that was pony rides. I think my aunty and uncle had thought of everything. Jack did not want to ride a pony, so he fed one instead. Luke lasted about thirty seconds before he freaked out, at least the other kids enjoyed the pony rides.

Soon the morning had flown by, and it was time to have a barbecue lunch. We all went inside, and Jack sat in the lounge room on the floor just playing with his new fire truck. He was happy with the food that he had, which was his chips and some carob strawberries and grapes Colin's daughter had made him. I had brought him an organic veggie burger for lunch. The day had been fantastic so far, with Uncle Colin also having heaps of gifts for the children, which were handed out by a giant fluffy dog (Colin's son in a dog costume).

Uncle Colin gave a short speech, which of course made me tear up again, as you do. We all started dancing, and Jack was having a laugh at the giant dancing dog. The kids loved the dog and wanted photos with him. They enjoyed hugging him and occasionally jumping on him.

It was eventually time to go, because we had an appointment to have our professional photos done. Although I had been worried about the kids getting tired, they were doing really well so far. As we left and packed all our gear into the car, what was I to say to my aunty and uncle...thank you? That just didn't seem enough, but that's all I could say. Those were the only words that told them exactly how I felt. It had been a perfect day, and they had gone to so much trouble and effort for my beautiful son Jack. I could never have dreamed up a party like this for him.

Thank you!

The gardens where we were having our photos was a good half an hour away, and both Jack and Luke fell asleep in the car, which was fantastic. Perfect actually, they would wake up happy and ready to go for the next adventure. We were a little early at the gardens and so we just sat there letting the boys have a well-earned rest. The rest of the family were slowly showing up, and the photographer was also, but I decided to wait a little bit longer before waking the boys up because the photographer wanted to have a good look around first.

The photos went well. The photographer grouped us and took all the photos we asked for. She even did some action shots while we were all mucking around. We had to keep busy while some of the family had their photos taken individually, so we had a ball and some cars to mess about with. The kids enjoyed picking up all the big leaves and running through the enormous trees. The trees were so old, and the roots were massive coming out of the ground. We climbed over them and hid in some of the trunks. We had great fun.

The session took quite some time, but for most of it the kids were exceptional, and I couldn't wait to see the final result. It had been a big day for all of us. I was so happy, because you know that it's going to be a big one, and you prepare emotionally and physically for it. When the kids are this good, it makes it so much easier.

It had been a perfect day!

CHAPTER 26

What is an angel? Our beautiful angels are our light that guides and protects us throughout our journey in this world. I would be lost without them. But sometimes all you have to do is look deep into the eyes of people here on earth and you just know that they were chosen to be here, crossing our paths at a certain time. They too are our angels. They glow.

Jack started to look healthy, although he never looked like he had any fat on him ever. His hair was starting to grow back, everywhere except where his radiotherapy treatment had hit.

Anthony, the two boys, and I went up to Samuel House. On our first night, Nansie, Poppie, and my niece Joey, who was nine, stayed as well. Jack just adored Joey, and she always played with him lovingly. We all played lots of games together.

That night Amanda rang me. We were just chatting, and I told her that Jack had started looking quite good. He was running around the house and playing in the big massive toy room happily and full of life.

"That's because he is getting better!" she said to me.

It was so uplifting to hear someone say that, even though deep down it was hard to change the knowledge that we were told that Jack didn't have much more time with us. It was nice that someone had hope and faith that it was possible to still help him, to still save him.

We had a really fun night, and it was great to see Jack and Joey having fun with the pinball machine, pool table, and hockey table. There were loads of books and also board games to play, which we did till we all went to bed that night. Nansie, Poppie, and Joey left us the next morning.

We decided to go to a wooden toy shop we had missed going to the last time that we were here. It was a great deal smaller that I had imagined, but it was fun having a little look around. Jack chose a few items like a wooden dice to throw around, a couple of wooden seed planters for Pa and our neighbour Peter, and a game that was a wooden circle the size of a dinner plate with holes in it that fitted a whole bunch of marbles. Jack loved marbles, and I believe that he was playing with marbles since he was just under two years old. He never put anything in his mouth, and he understood that they never were to be put anywhere. Luke was the one we were going to have to watch. He was terrible for that.

We met Aunty Jenny at the wooden toy shop, as she had decided to take a couple of days off and drive up to join us. We got our much-loved bakery products for lunch, and Aunty Jenny had brought up some favourites from a local butcher so that we could have a well-earned barbecue tea. We went back to the house, where Jack sat at the table and played with his new toy. It was a perfect choice for him.

The day went on and all went well, but by the afternoon Jack started getting a little weird. He was really full-on and aggravated. He was getting me stressed, and I felt unable to control him. He was obsessed with eating his green grapes covered in carob. I remember Amanda saying that everything, no matter what food it was, should be eaten in moderation. I was worried because all he wanted to eat was the grapes, even for his dinner.

Jack sat on the sink with Anthony and helped him peel prawns while I was busy stuffing my face with any yummy food I could get my hands on. It was like I was rewarding myself for just coping after each hard moment I was dealt. With the lives we were living, that seemed like it was all of the time.

Anthony noticed that Jack's speech had become slurred while he was helping with the prawns, and he was really tired. He had refused resting for the day, so it was understandable that he was completely exhausted. Aunty Jenny and I took Jack down to the playground, which turned into a complete meltdown. Jack was agitated, and I was unable to control him, so I just took him back up to the house.

He screamed for more grapes, which I hesitantly gave him. He ate them and then fell asleep on the couch sitting up. He was exhausted, and it was only around five in the evening.

We decided to put him to bed and let him sleep. Anthony carried him to the big bed in the main room where Jack always slept in between both of us. When Anthony got him to the bed, he awoke a little and started becoming agitated again. I left Anthony lying in bed with Jack, but I could hear that he was struggling to get Jack to sleep.

It wasn't long before Anthony called out to me, and I went in to find Jack crying. He had vomited all over the bed. I grabbed him and started to rock him and try to comfort him. He was so upset, and it made me worry, although it felt like those times when kids get woken up and they are really grumpy and upset because of it.

"Do you want a bath or a shower, Jack?" I kept asking him, but he just said no.

I somehow ended up sitting in the bathroom on the top of the toilet seat just rocking him. Every question I asked him got a "no!" and a bunch of tears. He held me so tight, but slowly he calmed down. I just kept rocking him and rocking him until he once again fell asleep. It was strange to me that he only said no. Somehow it felt like it was the only thing he was able to get out.

My poor baby, I just didn't know how he was feeling. Anthony had said he wasn't himself today, and we gave him all the prescribed medication to help him in case he was in any pain. I slowly put him to bed and tucked him in. Aunty Jenny and Anthony began cooking the tea on the barbecue, and I had a shower. I rang Nansie to tell her that Jack was not right and that he was in bed now.

I liked to always check on the kids constantly while they slept, even to a point that it was obsessive. My head said that I should go and check on Jack ... but I didn't. I was exhausted, and I didn't want to wake him. Instead I went into the big massive toy room and played the pinball for a little while.

Just one more game, I kept telling myself. Even thought my head kept telling me to go to Jack.

Finally, I stopped. This time, I listened to that voice in my head. I went to see if Jack was still asleep. I went in and saw him up on his knees on the bed.

"Hey buddy! You okay?"

Jack was just staring into nothing, with no expression on his face. His breathing was weird; it was wrong. I grabbed him and held him tight on my lap on the end of the bed.

"Jack, talk to me, are you okay?" I said forcefully, but he just managed small grunts, like he was trying to tell me, but he couldn't. His arm rose into the air as if he was trying to catch something that wasn't there. His eyes were not focusing. They weren't right.

"Jenny!" I screamed. "Get Anthony to call someone. Something is wrong!"

I heard her acknowledge me, and Anthony ran in.

"Call Dr. Marlene, call someone," I screamed. "It's not right, he's not right!"

"I'm going to push the emergency button! Should I push it?" Anthony yelled.

"Yes, push it! Push it!"

Anthony ran out and pushed the emergency button on the kitchen wall, and there was someone talking to us within seconds. I could hear what the female voice was saying from the bedroom because it was on a speaker. Jack was struggling to breathe; it was like he was forgetting how to. I just held him tight and told him how he should be breathing.

"Come on buddy, it's in and then out, in and then out, just keep breathing, buddy!" I knew he was listening to me because his breathing slowly became better.

Anthony came in and helped me to put Jack on his side on the bed and position him just as the woman had told us to over the speakerphone. It felt like forever. Luckily, Luke was in his playpen just playing, and Aunty Jenny was watching for the ambulance. She moved her car quickly out of the steep driveway, and we were concerned about how the ambulance would cope with getting up and down it. We just continued to stroke Jack's beautiful face and tell him how much we loved him and that he was all right because we were here with him.

The paramedics came, asked us lots of questions and hooked Jack up to many different gadgets. We informed Nansie and Ma, and Nansie decided that she was coming up to see Jack straight away, even though it was over a forty-five-minute drive. I wasn't sure what was going to happen to us all, but she was adamant that she would come.

I watched everything that was being done to my Jack. The paramedics were very soft-speaking and wonderful people, I must say. I just felt like everything was so slow. It took so long.

Hurry up! Hurry up he needs help! I thought.

They had managed to get Jack into the back of the ambulance, and as we left, we remembered to take all our identifications, knowing that we might need them for the hospital. We gave Aunty Jenny a quick rundown of what to do with Luke, and she was confident to take care of him. Anthony and I hopped into the back of the ambulance and we were off to the closest hospital in town. Strangely, just like everything else, it felt like the trip was an eternity.

We arrived at the hospital, and the staff brought Jack into one of the emergency areas, where a male doctor went through all the same questions with us as the paramedics had. I explained everything that had happened, and as they spoke to each other, I would answer questions for them in case they got it wrong. It was important to get everything right to the second, for Jack.

Jack continued to have mild seizures, and it was becoming clearer as time went by that the doctor in charge was not familiar or comfortable with the situation that Jack was in. He rang the specialist hospital where Jack had completed all of his operations and treatment to speak to Jack's doctor. Anthony helped with the information, and finally the doctor on duty here chose to call two other local doctors in.

It was late now, and finally the two different doctors who had been called in to help us turned up, both in shorts and T-shirts as if they had been at the beach. Both were male and very tall and confident, happy too, in a good way. They glowed. They took over and I knew that now I could breathe maybe for just a moment.

The older one, out of the two began to check Jack's breathing. I saw him notice that the mask wasn't working that was over Jack's face, as it had pulled out of the wall. It should have been giving Jack his oxygen, but it wasn't. He ripped off Jack's oxygen mask and replaced it with a handheld one that he would pump himself. He had chosen to take over and make sure that Jack's breathing was in his hands only ... safe hands. He did this all swiftly, so we wouldn't notice, but I noticed.

Nansie and Poppie turned up. I was unsure of what was going to happen now, but a small part of me was able to let go, as I finally felt confident with the doctors who was with him. I was afraid that Jack had chosen to leave us sooner that we had expected. I could only think of how disciplined I had been with him, not letting him have any chocolate or donuts, and now would he have a chance to ever taste one again?

Why didn't I let him have a donut? Why didn't I let him have chocolate cake at Nansie's birthday?

The nurses were doing their best to explain things to us and get all the paperwork under control. Jack continued to have numerous seizures, and they were trying to get him stable. The wonderful people at the children's cancer charity who owned Samuel House rang to support us, telling us that they would pack up our gear from the house and take it back to our home. They had heard about what was going on because of the buzzer being pushed at the house. We were the only ones who had ever used it. It was our saviour.

We were told that there would be a helicopter coming from the city to pick Jack up and take him back to the specialist hospital where they knew him.

The question for us was, "Are we going with him?"

It took a while before we found out that there was enough space for both Anthony and I to ride with him back to the specialist hospital. Usually there wasn't enough room. We were very lucky, because a long drive back without Jack sounded like a nightmare. What if he passed while we weren't there?

The time just kept ticking by, and finally two people from the specialist hospital arrived, a doctor and a female nurse. The doctor was a male doctor who reminded me so much of the doctor who had helped us in emergency on our first day with Jack. They were very lovely and completely professional, doing the job with no hesitations or doubt...just what I needed! They took a long time to prepare Jack, but they did it so wonderfully.

The two male doctors from the country hospital finally stepped aside. Throughout this whole time there were many occasions the nurses had asked to step in to continue pumping Jack's oxygen manually to give the older doctor a break, but he refused. He continued to take care of Jack's breathing. It was like he had taken ownership of my little boy. This man would make sure that Jack had every chance he deserved.

Those two doctors had worked so well together. They both came over and spoke with me now that Jack was stable and with the medical staff from the specialist hospital. Smiling and speaking gently, they gave me encouragement. Even their eyes shone, and I knew that they had been sent to take care of us ... of our Jack. They were his angels for just a moment, a very important moment. I could never say in words how much they meant to me and my family, to Jack.

I believe in angels here on earth now, including those who don't even know it. There are angels in us. Maybe these two doctor's whole life journey had brought them here just for this moment and many others like this one. I thank you, my earth angels.

It was finally time to get Jack into the helicopter, and as we took the rough journey out to the tarmac, I was feeling extremely guilty and selfish. My main train of thought was fear of flying in the helicopter.

Will I be sick? I'm scared!

How could I be so selfish? What about my Jack and what he was suffering? *Get over it, girl, and have some faith.*

Nansie and Poppie drove back to the city, and we hopped into the helicopter trying to listen to the instructions from the pilot. The seat was a tiny pulldown, and we had to wear head equipment. I was freaking out, and as I turned to my left, I saw that Anthony was freaking out too. The space was very small. Jack lay in the centre with the doctor and nurse seated close to his side. Anthony and I were on either side of his head, staring down at him.

There was more paperwork to be done within the helicopter, which took our minds off of the flight. I could describe the ride as like being in the back of a bus, it wasn't as bad as I thought it was going to be. We had to land on the roof of the hospital in the city where Jack had his radiotherapy done, because it was the only one with a helicopter pad. Then Jack was transported in an ambulance to the specialist hospital. We were told that there was not enough room for us in the ambulance to ride with Jack, so we had to wait around for a taxi, which came not too long after.

What the hell? I freaking just want to stab someone in the eye right now!

We arrived at the specialist hospital, Nansie and Poppie and many others were there also. Luckily, Nansie told us that she had insisted that she wait by the emergency entrance to be there as Jack arrived. Anthony and I were still on our way at that time. Nansie walked with Jack to the elevator so that he was not alone for too long. The thought of him alone without anyone he knew was horrible. We had to wait for Jack to be put into a private room within the intensive care unit, which is never a great sign. We were allowed to have an overnight room to stay in once again if we needed it.

Nansie came over and gave me a hug and asked me, "How are you feeling?"

"Numb!" I answered. "Just numb!"

"Me too," she said.

I had no emotions going on at all ... nothing. My body was in survival mode once again, protecting me so that I could do what I had to do to protect Jack. I couldn't be aware and, on the ball, if I was crying and lying in a mess of sorrow on the ground. No, I had to do my job, and that was to be Jack's mother, his protector, and his guardian in this world. There was no time to stand there and ask why, no time to be sad and shed tears. He was still here with me, and as long as he was, I was never giving up on him.

We finally could go in and see him. He lay there so peacefully on the bed. He had a tube down his throat to support his breathing and there were many wires hooked up to different machines. My poor little Jack. He must have been so tired. I looked at him and for some reason it seemed wrong, life without him, Luke without his big brother. I felt like we should have had more time; I wasn't ready to give him up just yet. We hadn't tried enough.

A doctor who was on at the time very slowly and nicely told Anthony and I that Jack was not in the best position at the moment. The machine was doing the work for him. We just nodded and then stood by Jack's side and held his hand, kissed him, and ran our fingers through his beautiful hair.

Anthony's brother Brenton and Pa travelled up to Samuel House. They brought Aunty Jenny and Luke back home to our house, where her and Ma stayed and took care of Luke. They rang to keep in touch, but there wasn't much to tell just yet. Brenton and Pa then came to the hospital. We had left all our gear up at Samuel House and would somehow fetch it another day. It wasn't important right now. We knew that the children's cancer charity group had told us that they would do it for us, but that seemed wrong to ask them. Little did we know that our family and friends would come together and take care of it.

Jack's oncologist, Dr. Marlene, showed up, along with another female doctor we had come to know and a woman from palliative care. Basically, Dr. Marlene told us that Jack's signs were not good and that he wouldn't recover from this. He wouldn't wake up. His breathing was by the machine only, and if we turned off the machine, he would not be able to breathe for himself. He was on many drugs to keep him peaceful and also on dexamethasone, the steroid that helps to shrink swelling.

I began to cry, and I thanked Dr. Marlene for all her help and support through this whole journey with Jack. It was the very first time that I thought in my head that I might actually lose Jack forever. I cried because she had confirmed it.

The lady from palliative care commented that it would be better this way for Jack. She continued to explain how he could have lingered and started forgetting how to do everything, which for a child would have been frustrating and terrible for us to watch as parents. Everyone just seemed as if they knew everything, as if this happened all the time, every day. Well why didn't they know exactly what they were doing through all of Jack's treatment? They didn't, so why would they know everything now?

They all left, and I looked down at Jack and inside my head I spoke to him. It just didn't feel right. There wasn't a goodbye. There wasn't time for me to tell him everything. Luke would be alone.

You know what, Jack? They may act as if they know everything, but they don't, and they have proved that without a doubt. I love you, and if you want to let go, then let go. If you are tired, then be free. But if you want to fight with me and just try one more time, then let's do it together! I love you!

I was very tired, so I sat by Jack's bed holding onto the side bar while I rested my head on my arm. It was the early hours of the morning now, and I had begun to close my eyes. I slowly drifted away, and while I was in that process of nodding off, my head began to slide off my arm it was resting on and came down with a loud bang onto the side bar of Jack's bed. My head shot up quickly as both Nansie and Anthony looked at me in shock.

"Are you all right?" Nansie asked.

"Yes," I replied as we all chuckled.

It was nice to actually break the air with a bit of a laugh, even though it was on me. Brenton left, and Anthony and Pa decided to have two hours' rest in the room that was provided for us, while Nansie and I stayed. When they returned, I went and had a lay down. Nansie refused to leave Jack's side, which I felt guilty about. How was she still awake? I was completely exhausted.

The doctor who had travelled with Jack and us in the helicopter was continually checking Jack's machines, and while Anthony and I were together, we talked with him. We told him about what we had been told by the other doctors, that Jack probably wouldn't make it through.

He looked at us a little strangely and answered, "Well, Jack's trying to breathe for himself, and although the machine is supporting him, he is still breathing a small amount. As I see it, the machine is not doing everything. Jack is still trying to breathe. Let me show you."

He showed us the machine that indicated Jack's breathing, and he explained it to us so that we could see the difference between Jack and the machine.

"I believe that there is still a small chance that Jack will wake up. How he will be or for how long, I can't say, but he is still showing signs of trying."

There it was, a huge wind of fresh air, full of hope. This one man among many had chosen to tell us exactly what was happening. He explained things to us instead of just covering it over with the final bad news. He did not believe that it was all completely and utterly final, and all he was doing was reading the information in front of him.

This new day had started to tick by, and as it went through, I rang all of my friends and told them the bad news. I gave them the opportunity to say goodbye to Jack. Aunty Jenny and Ma were eager to come in to see Jack, and while the time ticked on and on, more and more people came. The hospital allowed us many people in the room because of the circumstances. They were sedating Jack momentarily, but as it wore off, he began to squirm a little.

I chose to hold Jack in my arms, even with all the wires coming off of him. He was just wrapped in a sheet. We had a Catholic priest come and give Jack his final prayers and blessings, as we all prayed together for Jack. The room was full of our friends and family, many crying as they looked over our special Jack. The only noises were the small sobs of sadness and the loud beep, beep, beep of the machine. Aunty Jenny had made it in to see us, and she took a seat. Luke was still with Ma.

The male nurse caring for Jack had decided that he would have to turn the machine off soon, as Jack was becoming agitated with the pipe down his throat. We asked that he just wait for Ma and Luke, because we didn't know how long Jack would survive without the machine supporting him. The doctor tried to hold off, but Jack was getting more and more agitated. The male nurse decided that he would have to take the pipe out then and there. Just as he did, Ma walked into the silent room with Luke in her arms.

The air pipe that had supported Jack's breathing for so long was pulled out with one quick pull, and as it came out, Jack woke up, opening his eyes up wide. He sat up tall on my lap looking around wide-eyed.

He asked, "What's that noise?" It was the machine beeping. "I want something to eat!" he declared.

Everyone was amazed and stunned for a moment, and then we were all laughing. Although he had no idea what was happening, Jack began to laugh too, because everyone else was laughing. And there he was, my Jack, sitting on me asking for food as if nothing had happened. I kissed him and looked around a room full of joyful faces.

Across from me sat my uncle Colin, a man who chose to only believe in things he could see and understand, things that were real. As I looked over at him, he smiled and just shrugged his shoulders, shaking his head. It was unexplainable, a miracle even. I'm not sure what it was; all I knew was that this once dim lifeless room now looked as though there was a party going on.

Aunty Jenny was blown away. She stood up smiling with tears running down her face. She stepped right up to Jack and shook her finger at him.

"Jack!" she said. "Don't you ever do that to me again!"

Jack laughed at her with his beautiful smile, and she gave him a big hug. Everyone wanted to kiss, hug, or high-five special little Jack, who had decided that he needed to play with everyone and have something to eat, the two most important things in the entire world. Oh, and milk.

It was amazing just sitting back watching him. It was like he fell asleep and woke up completely the same, happy and vibrant, free of cords and machines now. As Jack was surrounded by so many people, Nansie and I stepped out into the hall where I was just glowing with happiness. I didn't know how long I would have him for; all I knew was that I had him. I had this moment.

Little Joey, his cousin who had been with us and like everyone else had said her goodbyes to her little cousin and friend, was walking around in the hallway too.

"Do you have any questions, sweetheart, you want to ask?" I said to her.

She just shook her head and smiled. I wasn't sure what to do or say. She was one of Jack's closest friends. They had a connection that was precious and undeniably strong. I just gave her a cuddle while a million thoughts went through my head.

I have another chance, I thought.

But this time, I wanted Jack to enjoy everything in life. I was going to do all I could to save him and make him happy at the same time. The atmosphere was wonderful. All his doctors returned with amazed and shocked grins on their faces.

"What can we say?"

It was an absolute pleasure for me that they were wrong and that he was awake and happy. They said that the steroid dexamethasone they had given him had opened up this window of life for Jack, but was it just that? Maybe it was everything: God? Fate? Luck? All the healthy stuff we had poured into his body? The steroid? Who knows?

Some people were calling it a miracle, but to me, Jack being completely cured would be a miracle. Maybe I would just call this a great gift that God gave me, the gift of more time. I had more time with my son.

CHAPTER 27

The most precious commodity in this world is not gold. It is not a rare gem. It is not money of any kind. It is not real estate, stocks, bonds or any personal item that can be sold for a pretty penny. The most precious item you own is time. Once time is gone you can never get it back, so be careful with how much you give away to the wrong investments. Time is now, and it can be nothing more than a single moment. Live in the moment knowing that the past has gone, and the future can be anything you want it to be... if you invest your time in what it should be invested in.

A s the time went by, people slowly left the hospital, and Luke, who was happy no matter where or who he was with, had been taken home. Anthony went to get a few supplies, as we were going to be moved later on that afternoon to the chemotherapy ward for the night. Jack had begun to tire and chose to lay on the couch rather than his bed to have a nap. He was close to me.

I sat by his feet as he slept so peacefully, and alone, by myself, I found that I was addictively watching him breathe. In and out, in and out. I just couldn't help it. I couldn't turn away. Although he was strong and vibrant now, I couldn't stop remembering that he wasn't meant to be breathing at all by himself. It was a little shallower than normal, but for what he had just been through, it was strong ... in and out, in and out, just making sure that it would continue to be.

I had a feeling of fear as I sat there all by myself, wondering what would happen if he were to pass while by my side like this with me. I shouldn't have been worried. He was an amazing kid, and I had been given my chance to tell him just one more time how much I loved him. I stood up and stretched my legs, I went and stood in the doorway of the room.

Yesterday the hospital chaplain had come in and asked if he could give Jack a blessing, which was lovely of him, but we had already asked a priest from the Catholic church to do it, as I previously said. The hospital chaplain returned today to see how Jack was doing, and as he walked up to the doorway where I was standing, his heart dropped as he saw the empty bed. Saddened he held his hand out and asked how I was.

"We are fine, thank you. Jack is asleep on the couch over there where you can't see him." And I gave him a big smile. He stepped back with shock and walked around the empty bed to see Jack sound asleep.

"I'm so sorry. I saw the empty bed!" His amazement was like a gift he was unable to hold back. I told him what had happened, and he was overjoyed.

"Lazarus!" he said smiling and throwing his hands into the air full of praise. We had a laugh, and he left in awe, as many others had done already.

Anthony returned, and everything was peaceful. Jack was asleep, and soon we were to go up to the chemotherapy ward for the night. It was almost five o'clock. The doctor who had told us that Jack still had a chance had come in to see us. We couldn't stop thanking him. He had given me the hope that I needed to just believe that Jack would wake up, and he did.

Once again, I had seen an angel, a man who had given us a small gift and done all he could for Jack. From then on, I saw everyone as humans, equal. I saw them for their attitudes, hearts, souls, and minds. We all do silly things in our lives, and we are all judgemental as I was at the beginning of this journey, but a person's true self, no matter what, will always shine through in good and bad times. This is what I will choose to see and believe in from now on. God made us all the same, no matter how different we are.

The chemotherapy ward was so quiet. We had drawn the curtains and sat in the darkness. I was on the recliner with my legs up, and Jack rested on me sleeping. I wondered what kind of a night we would have tonight after Jack sleeping so much during the day. In the end it really didn't matter, as long as I had Jack.

Amanda had come to visit, as did my friend Sarah. Amanda brought in some special juice that she wanted Jack to drink, so she put it into the fridge as Sarah pulled up a chair by my feet. I began asking Amanda questions, because she was just so sure that Jack was getting better with all these natural remedies before this happened. She still seemed adamant that Jack would be fine.

A nurse came in with Jack's medication, which from now on, was going to increase. There were so many that he needed; painkillers, meds for seizures, and the steroid dexamethasone. There was only one for now, and that was the steroid. Jack hated this stuff. It made him vomit at times, but by the looks of things, it may have become his saviour.

The nurse wanted to stay and watch Jack take it, which meant waking him and giving him this horrible stuff. Then Amanda started on the nurse.

"What is it? What's it for? This is the stuff that is contaminating his little body. You don't have to give him that!"

The nurse was a little stunned and just came out with, "His doctor has written this for Jack to have, and so I am administering it."

I asked the nurse to give us a minute and to leave the medication with me so that I could try to wake him slowly, and she did. Sarah became agitated with Amanda, I could see.

I began to cry, "What am I supposed to do?" I asked. I felt trapped.

Sarah rubbed my legs up and down. I could see she felt helpless and angry, but she held it all in.

I said to Amanda, "You're telling me that all the medications the doctors are giving Jack are poisoning him, and yet I know that without it he could die right now. So, what do I do?"

Amanda shrugged her shoulders, sighed, and sat on the bed, "I guess you just have to do both."

We were all unsure of what to do. How could I say no to any medicine when it could stop Jack from having those seizures that seemed like they were never going to stop? The steroid that took away the inflammation from his brain, the anti-vomit, the painkillers? He must have been in so much pain. Which poison do I not give him?

And so, I woke him mildly, and I gave him his medication with a drink of the juice that Amanda had brought in, and he went back to sleep. There was, to me, no choice. I would have to monitor all his drugs like I had always done, and I would pump into him as much of the natural stuff that I could. He would eat healthy, but I was not going to stop him from eating a naughty thing here and there.

Today was now December 18. Yesterday I thought I was going to lose my Jack forever, before his next Christmas. Even though I didn't know how much longer I would have Jack for, he was going to have fun no matter what. That night, we put Jack into bed, and I slept on a recliner while Anthony slept on the fold-out bed. For some strange reason, we all slept well, even though I kept checking Jack's breathing every time I awoke.

The following morning was all about filling us in on what medications we had to give Jack at home, how much, and when. There was a lot. We administered his seizure medicine before we left the hospital, and then we were free to go. I was nervous to leave, but Anthony and I grabbed everything we could and just flew out of there. We got to our last corridor and ... oh no, Jack had a massive spew all over the floor, and it was red, which indicated it was his seizure medicine. I sat with Jack on a chair cuddling him while Anthony ran back to the ward to get advice. We were both up for the realisation that we might have to stay another night. Anthony returned and so did a cleaner.

"Let's go!" said Anthony.

"What about his medication?" I asked.

"He had it longer than half an hour ago, so we just give it to him again when he next needs it."

We left, and as we drove him home, Jack fell asleep again. I would turn and watch his breathing and sometimes for a moment I thought that he had stopped, but he hadn't. I felt his breathing was quite shallow, and I really was unsure of how long he could continue on. He was such a fighter. We returned home, where Nansie had been watching Luke. She was shocked to see that we had come home with Jack.

"They let you out?" she asked, concerned.

"I'm not sure how long we have him, Nansie," I said to her. "His breathing is weak."

"Shall we open all the presents under my tree today so that we know he has had a Christmas?"

"That's a great idea!"

So, Anthony, Jack, Luke, Nansie, and Poppie went up to Nansie's house. We took all the presents we had for Jack and put them under Nansie's tree as well. First, I had a long shower to wash off all the stress that was on my shoulders. I then walked down to Nansie's house, and Jack just went for it. He had a fantastic time ripping all the presents open, and Luke loved watching him. Luke played with the wrapping paper.

I decided that Santa Claus had to come early for Jack; he was going to come tonight, make a special trip just for Jack and Luke and drop off one last present. I had a friend of mine, Lee, get one of her friends to impersonate Santa Claus on the phone to Jack, and he told Jack that he was going to make a special delivery.

So that night, when we got the boys to sleep, I set up the freestanding piano that we had bought for them both. Nansie had one at her house, and they both loved playing it so much, especially Jack. I wasn't sure if I should set up the boys' Santa sacks, because if Christmas did finally come, I would have to buy everything again, but I put the presents in the sacks just in case. The next morning, Jack and Luke woke up and both came out to see what Santa had brought for them. Jack looked at the piano, which was cool, but he wanted to know what else Santa had left him. Nansie and I just looked at each other, and I slipped out of the room and returned with the full Santa sacks. I hid them behind the couch.

"What else?" Jack asked again.

"You will have to find it!" I said.

Jack looked around, and then he found the sacks behind the couch ... yay! We sat both boys on the rug with their sacks. Anthony filmed and took photos. I could see Jack's face. It had a *that's what I'm talking about* look on it. Ratbag!

We had a great day at home playing with all the new toys. Jack was becoming tired a lot more easily, which was understandable for all that he had been through. It was hard trying to get into a routine with all his foods and his medications; I still wanted him to be really healthy, or as healthy as he could be without feeling like he was missing out on anything. We continued with all the natural products as best as we could, his Western medications we gave to him in their correct specifications. There were times when he had just had enough, so I would forfeit some natural items but then try again later. Jack was so good, though. He would normally just take it if we gave it to him.

CHAPTER 28

You are born into this world as unconditional love from unconditional love, meaning that you are loved unconditionally just because you exist. No matter what circumstances you are born into upon this planet, nothing can ever change the fact that you are made up of that love, born of that love and will always be that kind of love.

The nights had begun to take their toll as Jack was back sleeping between us. The medications sometimes had bad side effects on him. He would get up onto his hands and knees and crawl to the edge of the bed, almost falling off. I would wake him just in time to stop him. He was agitated at night, finding it hard to fall asleep. Anthony and I would take it in turns to lay with him until he did fall asleep, which could take up to two hours. It was exhausting.

Jack's behaviour was sometimes difficult to handle. It was hard not to get frustrated with him. You knew that it was the drugs and that it really wasn't him, but you just couldn't help trying to get him to do things by yelling. It didn't work.

One night we just put both the boys in the car and drove. We drove for almost an hour and a half before Jack finally closed his eyes and fell asleep. Luke had lost the battle within minutes, but Jack just couldn't. It actually was a more relaxing change to the night-time ritual we had been having. We were looking at investigating his medications, which we kept on trying to get right, tweaking them so the side effects would reduce. We continually had conversations with our doctors, and they kept on giving us feedback and ideas of what to do.

The day before Christmas Eve, I had decided that I would go out with Aunty Jenny and redo all the boys Christmas presents, even the Santa Claus ones. They had to still have a Christmas Day. It was a miracle that we would have Jack after all that we had been through. I loved spoiling him, and even though our bank account had never been so low, I felt a duty to him to make this the best time ever.

We went to a big well-known toy shop that night and grabbed presents for the boys. Aunty Jenny was so wonderful and paid for half of the products I was getting. I will never forget all she did for us, ever. I know that the boys would not have had another Christmas if she hadn't offered to help us out that day.

We went home, and I decided that I was going to wrap each of the Santa Claus presents individually so that Jack would have not only his to unwrap but Luke's as well. Luke was not interested in unwrapping presents just yet, only playing with the wrapping paper. Tomorrow night we were having all my family over for Christmas Eve. We thought it would be best at our house with Jack, and it would give everyone a chance to see him and spend some quality time together.

Yes, Christmas Eve was hard! Jack had a great time with all the kids; he loved having people in the pool while he threw the small plastic balls in at them. It was hard because you always had to keep yourself close to him even though there were lots of people around. You had to keep a watch on him and the way he was tracking.

Of course, there was Luke too. He was still young and into everything. It was becoming quite exhausting to still have to entertain and keep the celebrations going. My sister-in-law Kerry told me that she had never seen me get rattled with the kids until that night, but you can only take so much. As the night went on, it just became harder and harder trying to negotiate with Jack. He was having pains in his stomach and they were getting worse.

We rang the hospital, and they felt that because of all his medications, he was becoming constipated. We had been given a drug for that too, which we gave him as well. It was late, and Jack was slowly settling down after much screaming from his stomach cramps and his big day. He finally fell asleep and slept well. I think that the drugs and the levels we were giving him were slowly working out, making it a little better throughout the night.

The next morning was great! Jack was so excited about opening all the presents one by one from Santa, and he loved that he could open some of Luke's as well. The whole morning went well, as Jack relieved himself a little bit with his tummy pains, making himself feel a bit better. He was so happy and full of joy when we went to Nansie's to open all the other presents.

For me, this was a great start to a wonderful Christmas. It didn't matter how it went along, we would just track the day with how Jack was feeling. After the morning present rip-fest at Nansie's house, we brought them all home and Jack was ready for a rest. Nansie was getting lunch ready, and although Jack was sleeping soundly, and time was ticking past lunchtime, it didn't matter. We would wait until Jack was ready before we were up and off again.

Lunch was fun, and Jack got to drink from this small crystal port glass that had his juice in it. He would cheer each of us by hitting his glass onto ours and then sipping from it. We wore silly paper hats that we pulled from the bonbon we had cracked open, and we shared the jokes we found inside. They were always good for a laugh. We saved some presents, so Jack could undo some more. We wanted the day to last as long as it could.

Jack was doing well with all his medications and his natural products too, and it had been a few days since he had vomited. Christmas Day was slowly coming to an end, and Jack was exhausted. He was calming down, which meant all the hard work with tweaking his drugs was paying off. The old Jack was coming back.

He was asleep on the couch but still waking in some pain, and although we had already administered morphine at seven thirty, we rang the hospital at now ten at night and they advised us to give another 0.6 ml. Jack then settled when we put him to bed, and I was so happy with how the day went. Jack had an amazing time. What a special day to know that he was here with us. Christmas would have been a sad time if we had lost him a week ago.

During the next week, we had a few days of excitement coming up, with Anthony's birthday on December 27 and New Year's Eve, which was Luke's first birthday. Jack was ill in the morning of Anthony's birthday, as the day before was the last of his steroid. He vomited twice, and we administered his morphine along with his paracetamol. He had started to sleep a great deal longer in the mornings, which worried me. Would this cause vomiting when he awoke after lying on his head for so long asleep?

The lady who had started to take care of Jack from the palliative care unit was due to come over the morning of the 29th at ten o'clock, which she did do, but Jack was still fast asleep in our bed. We asked her a whole bunch of questions, which she answered. It seemed all was well with his medications, and now that the steroid was finished, he was so much more settled. He was peaceful. Her opinion came down to everything adding up to this being normal: Jack sleeping in. We just let it be and hoped that he would wake up feeling okay.

On Luke's first birthday, Nansie was not well and was unable to see Luke. It was important that no one got sick, especially with Jack being so unwell at the moment. Our nights were calming down now, as we found peace with his medications, which was difficult enough. We didn't want any added viruses.

I knew that Nansie would be disappointed because she couldn't come over, so we decided to open the presents with Poppie at our house and Nansie on the phone, and we cut the cake, too, singing "Happy Birthday." Jack loved birthdays. He loved getting a piece of cake at any time and sticking a candle in it just to sing "Happy birthday to ..." anyone. It was fun.

We decided to go and sleep that night at Anthony's parents' house. We had been experiencing some loud music from the neighbours next door to us, which had been going on for some time now, and Anthony was sick of it. We drove up to Ma and Pa's house for the night because we knew that our noisy neighbours would be having a big party. That night, of course, for the first time in years, Anthony's parents' neighbours had a massive New Year's Eve party. We couldn't believe it!

Anthony spent the night in the single bed with Luke in a port-a-cot in the same room. I had Jack on a double blow-up bed with me in the back-lounge room, where I listened to the party all night. Jack had a great night's sleep and didn't wake up until eleven twenty the following morning, which means I had a bit of a sleep-in too. I got up earlier than Jack and left him there to sleep. He was so peaceful. His late sleep-ins were something that I did worry a little bit about, knowing very well that it was all part of this disease eating away at him.

CHAPTER 29

Miracles are real! Don't think that they always come big and bold, they come small as well. See all the wonderful miracles in this world, some are happening every day. From the tiniest of miracles comes great hope and belief that all things are possible. Hope is the strength that is needed in all dire moments. Hope calls to miracles to come to fruition.

S lowly, each day he woke a bit earlier, and after another week he had gotten back to a normal eight o'clock rise. He would vomit once every two days, but he was taking most of his medications and natural products really well. He was on ondansetron (anti-vomit), Tegretol (seizures), oxycodone (pain), paracetamol (pain), Phenergan (nausea), MS Contin (pain), lactulose (bowels), and the natural products Triplex, Vitamin C,

V.M-Tech products, sea salt drops, Essiac, Rhomanga, pawpaw juice, bovine cartilage, and olive leaf extract. We were also doing the Zapper. Remember, some of these things were up to three times daily.

Aunty Jenny had come across someone who was having Indian Ayurveda massage by a man who lived not far from us. Jenny gave me the man's name, and although she was not sure how it could help or if it would work, she gave it to me anyway.

"Anything's worth a shot!" she said, and she was right.

I phoned the number and had a very long chat with the wife of this man, Peter, who did the massage. She was very lovely to talk to, so after discussing Jack, we booked in a couple of appointments. Jenny wanted to go to the first one just to check it out.

Now, just to let you know, I've never done anything at all with Jack unless I had some sort of knowledge about it. Every drug and natural product he was on or had ever been on I had looked up. I went onto the Internet to find out about this. It was different from anything I had ever done before, but it had come to the point where I had to try anything. I was not giving up, and the more things I tried, the better my odds for Jack could be.

We looked for a car park near the place, and it ended up that I drove straight past it, so I settled on a car park down a side road that was a small walk. I parked a little up the road because there was a small café further down that I didn't want to park in front of. I stopped the car, and as I went around to get Jack out of the car, I saw the strangest thing! Along the edging of the footpath, in large capital letters, was "JACK." Someone had written it obviously when the cement was wet, and goodness knows how long ago. Jack practically stepped out of the car onto it!

His name was there as if he had been here before and written it himself. The strange thing about it was that I was going to park in a different place but kept changing my mind until I got to here. I parked here exactly where Jack stepped out of the car. I got my phone and took a photo of it. For me, it was like someone drawing a map for me. Jack was meant to come here, for whatever reason.

When we got to the Ayurveda place, we had our doubts. We walked through the door, and it was old and dirty looking. We sat there and waited in the two chairs available feeling slightly odd and out of place. There was nobody at the reception desk, but we could hear muffled voices from one of the two doors in front of us.

One of the doors opened and out walked a bald woman dressed in monk-type clothing wrapped around her. She smiled and began to speak with us, she was very lovely, she had just had an appointment with Peter.

Then out came Peter. He was dressed in long cotton beige pants and a long tunic-style matching top. He had no shoes on, and his hair was long and grey. He was exactly what we thought he would probably look like. Jenny and I just looked at each other and smiled. Jack was having a great time talking to the female monk; she waved to him as she left.

"Hi, you must be Jack!" Peter said as he shook Jack's hand. "Would you like to come in?"

"Sure!" said Jack. We all went in.

Aunty Jenny and I sat on a chair while he got Jack to lie down on the bed. Jack didn't really want to at first, but Peter let him sit up while looking him over. We discussed Jack in full and what had happened to him and his treatments. Jack lay down on the bed now without a care. Peter placed his hands over Jack's body, not touching him, and closed his eyes. Peter was very positive that Jack had every chance to be well again, which gave me a little spark in my heart. He told me that Jack's aura was very strong and very bright, which was amazing to hear after all that Jack had been through.

"Man, this kid is going to rule the world!" he said as he smiled.

I smiled back and realised what he had said. Peter was practically telling me that Jack's aura was so great and so strong that he was going to be someone of importance in this world. Peter had no worries for Jack, to the point that in our following appointments, I felt like Peter couldn't understand my concerns for Jack's illness, like they weren't necessary.

"You need to stop worrying and relax. You should be having a treatment from me too!" he said to me, but I refused. This wasn't about me, I had one focus in my life, and that was to get Jack well again.

Peter would not accept any money for Jack's treatments, which blew me away. He told me that he just couldn't, that it wouldn't be right, which was fantastic. Our money was slowly becoming non-existent with all the food and the products I had been buying, trying to make everything Jack ate organic and fresh.

Peter would massage Jack with oils once a week, and he told me to do it also with the sea salts he provided, so every night I added that into our daily routine. They were to be rubbed down his spine and, on his neck, and head; this was supposed to help draw out the illness.

We also had him on mag-phos (magnesium phosphate), which would help with Jack's twitching at night-time; one of the main reasons he found it hard to go to sleep at night. He would be drifting off, and then his body would twitch and wake him up. The final thing we would give him was bicarb. In the good old days, they would take bicarb to turn the body from acidic to alkaline. One of the reasons for cancer is an acidic body caused by our world, food, environment ... everything! So, Jack got a very small amount of that a day too. The list went on.

It wasn't hard to add those small things, because I told Jack that the mag-phos tablets were a small white lolly and he could have it as a treat. It worked! I can't believe it.

Peter also gave Jack a small pink stone as a gift and told him to put it under his pillow at night-time. I had no idea what it was or what it would do, but I put it under his pillow every night just as Peter had said to do.

Jack seemed to be going along quite nicely. He now woke at a normal time every morning and was coping well with all his medications. Nansie had made it a ritual to come down and help me with the two boys on Monday, Tuesday, Wednesday, and Friday mornings at eight fifteen. Ma would come down on Thursdays to do the same. It was such a great help to have them there throughout the day, as it was difficult taking care of both the boys while Jack was unwell and Anthony at work fulltime. Luke was still young and getting into everything.

Jack had his little blue table and chairs he would sit at to eat his meals and snacks on. He loved eating and was always looking for food, but his little brother Luke loved to annoy him. He would crawl over, pull himself up with the table, and try to steal Jack's food or even the toys he had at the time. Jack would give out this unbelievable squeal, and we would have to remove Luke, but man, it was so funny watching Luke trying so hard to get anything from his brother. His eyes were full of wonder and ideas, as if he were planning his every move to just get a little closer.

All day every day we would play together. We would take the boys out shopping and to playgrounds and have loads of fun. Don't all kids just want to have fun? So, we did.

Whenever I had an appointment for Jack with the Ayurveda massage man Peter, Nansie would stay home with Luke. Sometimes Poppie would come with Jack and I. Every time I saw Peter, I had a million questions for him. I told him that I was planning on getting Jack another MRI scan because of all the natural things I had been giving him, and with all the positive feedback, I was looking forward to it. My dream was that the cancer would be completely gone. I had been reading books about people's cancer just disappearing after choosing a natural way to fight the disease. Peter was always positive, saying that Jack's aura was still so strong and bright, so it gave me great hope for this MRI.

"I don't care about the MRI or what it says," said Peter. "It means nothing to me! Let's just focus on Jack getting better. I have never lost a patient who has cancer who has not had chemotherapy."

Peter continued to work on Jack, and his words spun inside my head. He had never lost anyone with cancer who had come to see him, but then I thought about it more and more until I realised what he had actually said. He hadn't lost anyone with cancer who *had not* had chemotherapy. Well, Jack had chemotherapy for a very long time and radiotherapy, so what on earth did that mean?

Have I poisoned him? Have I chosen the wrong way to go about his cancer? Is he going to die because he has had the chemotherapy?

My mind was spinning. I think Peter didn't want me to have the MRI, probably because it was more harmful drugs we would be putting into

Jack, but I wanted to know if any of this natural stuff had been working at all.

We continued to see Peter about twice a week, and I noticed that Jack had been vomiting at least once a day now. I was so afraid to take Jack out because of his vomiting, although I carried a collapsible vomit bag from the hospital with me in my handbag at all times.

Was it the cancer making Jack vomit more often?

Peter assured me that the vomiting was a good sign for Jack and that the more he vomited, the more of the crap that was inside his body was coming out. If Jack had cancer anywhere else in his body than his brain, then I might have believed him. His words were comforting to me, yes, but the tumour had been sitting on the part of the brain where it touched the point that would make you vomit.

Everything continued day by day. It was the only way I was able to keep going, just living one moment at a time, doing what needed to be done so that the world was peaceful to some extent. I tried to never really think too much about it all, otherwise I probably would have just collapsed.

There were moments, when I was on my own that the tears were just uncontrollable and the anger of it all was explosive. I remember one day that will always stay with me. Little Luke was ready for a nap, and as I rocked him in the rocking chair, Jack just continued to disrupt him and wake him. The only thing in my mind was that I needed this child asleep. I had been waiting all morning, and though I repeatedly told Jack to leave the room, he just continued to be even more annoying.

I think that I actually felt my blood boiling within my skin, and I let it rip! I stood up and screamed at him like I had never screamed before, with my whole body pounding so loudly that my ears were throbbing. I could hardly breathe. That first moment when my mouth opened, and my words blew out, the look on Jack's face was something I will never forget. His little body shook with fear just from my voice, and he slithered down a little along the wall and then ran off.

That moment I closed my eyes, turned around, gently placed Luke in his cot awake, and closed the door. I went down the hallway to where Jack stood scared and sad. I walked up to him with his eyes locked on mine, and I knelt down to him.

"Mummy is so sorry, Jack. I should never have yelled at you!"

He emotionally replied, "No, you shouldn't yell at me, Mummy!" His tears were like daggers in my heart.

"Can you forgive Mummy?" He nodded, and I just gave him a great big hug. "Mummy just gets mad sometimes, and I'm sorry, my love. I love you."

"That's okay, Mummy, I love you too."

"I'm going to check on Luke," I told him.

Jack smiled, and I gave him another hug. He ran off to play without a care. I went to check on Luke, and to my surprise, he was sound asleep. Thank God!

I know that it just became too much for me to bear, and I know that it's just my humanness, but it was not okay to take it out on Jack. To this day, I am so glad that the moment I did that horrible yelling I simply stopped, composed myself, and apologised. I would never have forgiven myself if I had just let it go. We all make mistakes, and especially under such great pressure, but when it happens it must be fixed. I was wrong, and I was sorry.

CHAPTER 30

Do not ever regret or curse an honest mistake or bad decision you have made in the past. It has set your learning and your path. You are meant to be here. Just focus and try something different. I can never understand good people who do not own up to their mistakes or those who punish themselves so badly for them. It is human and wonderful to make our small life mistakes. We learn and grow from them. How else can you learn and grow? Information is studied through books, but life, true life, is learned this way.

Anthony and I had chosen to go through with the MRI because we truly believed that with all the efforts and natural medicines we had given Jack, there would be a significant improvement to his disease. We had really pumped him hard, even though we still had to give him the Western medications. I believed that I had found a way to cure him.

The morning was very positive. Ma was so excited about seeing the results; she too believed not only that he would be better but that he would be completely cured. For me, I just wanted a small positive, a slight reversal in the disease. That's all I needed to continue forward.

It was a new year, and I thought that if Jack made it to his birthday at the end of July, he would be on the way to recovery. They had already told us that he should have died in December, and yet he was still here with us, at the end of February, having a great time.

The day went as it normally did, and probably as smoothly as it could have gone. We had an appointment with Dr. Marlene the following day. It was so strange to have such a great feeling about the MRI. It was something I had never had before.

We got called in to Dr. Marlene's office, and she put up Jack's scans on the light board and showed them to us. She explained them once again very carefully and precisely. She was not surprised to see that Jack's brain and spinal fluids had now started to thicken up and become like the consistency of honey instead of a smooth watery fluid. The scan was showing nothing but how much worse the cancer had become. My belief for a cure had been suffocated by the truth that my son was dying, and quickly.

I don't know if I can describe to you how I felt. I had come so far and believed so much. I never gave up. This was the point, I think, that Anthony finally decided that the reality was that we were going to lose Jack. How could I as a mother decide to give up? If his heart was beating and he drew breath, then for me there was still a chance.

We went back to Ma's house, where we told her the results and I just started to cry. It had just become too much. To give all that you had and so much more, only wanting a small moment of hope, just anything, and never getting it. Jack did what he did best, he looked at me with his kind eyes and put his hand onto my face.

"Mummy, what's wrong?"

He was so worried about me and why I was crying. That was Jack. His love was so pure and endless. Every day he was going through excruciating pain and suffering, and yet there he was with his soft little hand on my cheek, asking me if I was all right. His face glowed, and his eyes were full of wisdom. I just told him that Mummy was fine.

The thing that scared me the most about Jack was that he was different. He wasn't like a normal kid; he had too much knowledge of life to have never been here before. He looked at me sometimes like he knew what was going on, but I think he had always known. I was the one catching up all the time.

Nansie had told me once about when Jack was playing at her house and he just came out and said, "Guess what, Nansie! I'm going to heaven!"

Nansie told me that although she was shocked, Jack was happy and excited about it. The photos we took of him would have that camera flash shine in so many of them. It scared me. He glowed so much that he shone in the photos. I knew he was an angel. I knew he was trying to teach me something, but unless it was how to cure cancer, I didn't want to listen.

We returned to see Peter and to continue with his therapy, and I told him about the MRI results. I knew that he did not want me to have the MRI done, but I was so positive about it; I needed to see it. Maybe this was my downfall, that I always needed to have proof and to be in complete control.

The appointment with Peter was very different that day. I asked him how he felt about Jack now that the MRI results had shown that the cancer had become worse. Was Jack's aura still as strong as before? He told me yes, but there was a stumbling in his voice and a great deal of doubt in his eyes. That moment, I knew that Peter had given up. There was something he could see that he had not seen before. Or was it that because I had found out how bad the results appeared, he knew himself that Jack would not survive?

This was the last time we ever went to see Peter. Jack was vomiting so much that it was hard to even get him out of the house. We just didn't know when he would be sick. I still continued everything that had been taught to me by Peter every day.

There was a day when we went out shopping and once again gave Jack his rides, he loved them. This time when we got to the end of the shopping centre, we put Luke and Jack on a bright yellow car. After it began, Jack's face dropped, and he put his arms out with a small hint of fear in his eyes.

Nansie grabbed him off, and I thought he may have felt sick, but he didn't vomit. Then Luke began to cry, and so I took him off the ride. Jack must have felt uneasy on the ride for some reason. This was our last time out in the world, things had just become too scary.

I raced home that day thinking Jack might need seizure medication, you could see in his face that he wasn't quite right, but we ended up getting through it without any medications. I received a speeding fine in the mail after racing home that day. Such is life!

Luke knew something was wrong with Jack on that ride, I could see it. Whatever Jack felt on that ride, it made Luke afraid. Luke has never gone on a shopping centre ride ever again. He cries every time.

Jack had started to have these mild weird moments where he would become instantly tired or ill. His face would just have this complete blankness to it, and I knew straight away to grab a bucket and then to grab him.

You would yell his name "Jack! Are you all right?" and there would be nothing from him. Then there was a massive vomit, and then he would just scream as he came back to us.

Once he was eating when it happened, and he started choking. I was yelling at him to spit out his food, but he was motionless. Luckily, up came a vomit and cleared his throat and mouth of everything, and bang! he was back to screaming for a moment and then off to play.

Sometimes these episodes got too much for him, and he would need to rest for a while. To me, it was like complete exhaustion. His little body could only deal with so much now, and a rest was needed to revive him. He was starting to sleep more each day, and the vomiting was slowly getting worse. His little body was becoming thinner and frailer.

It was a blessing to me that Nansie came four days of the week and Ma came on Thursdays to help me with Jack. It was such a relief to have that extra set of hands. Life was very unpredictable.

I continued to tell myself each day that I would do my best to get as many natural healing products into Jack, have a great time with him and Luke, and just play. All I had to do was get him to his birthday. If he made it to July, then I was sure that we were on the right road. Jack and I would plan his birthday party, a superhero one, which I felt was appropriate. He would be four then.

It was now the beginning of April. We had gone about fifteen weeks after that horrible moment of the doctors telling us that Jack would pass away, because he could not breathe without the machine. It was also seventeen weeks from when they told us Jack had relapsed and only had a maximum of twelve weeks left to live. It was only another fifteen weeks to his birthday. Surely, we could keep going.

On Wednesday, April 8, we did a whole bunch of painting. Jack loved to paint, and so this time I decided to get him to do a handprint and footprint for me. We got so messy, but I now had his impressions on paper, which I had never done before.

This coming Sunday was Easter, and Jack was so excited, he couldn't wait! He loved chocolate and he loved to play games, so it was perfect. We talked about hunting for Easter eggs and eating chocolate all day.

As I lay with Jack on Friday night and he fell asleep in our bed, I had the feeling that he had become so tired. The belief that I just had to get him to his birthday had become a false hope once again, and I knew that he was slowly becoming worse every day. The signs of his body shutting down were prominent. He started to forget his colours and other details that he knew so well.

I rubbed my nose into his hair, which I loved to do because it was so soft, and I sang a song to him while he slept. At that moment, I knew. I prayed to Mary, the mother of Jesus, as she was the only one I felt could relate to my situation at the time. She had lost her son to a long and painful death, and so she could intercede with God on my behalf.

I prayed, "Dear Mary, if it is to be that Jack will be taken from me, then please give him the best weekend and Easter that he could possibly have, and then take him. But if there is a miracle and he is to stay, then cure him … now!"

On Sunday morning, Jack and Luke each woke to a basket full of chocolates left by the Easter Bunny. They were throwing them and eating them at five in the morning. Luke thought they were balls and started to throw them across the room, just missing Jack's head! They were laughing and having a great time.

Jack looked like he was in really good spirits. He was full of energy and ready to have a great big fun day full of chocolate. We went to Nansie's house, and so did my brother's family, Poppie, my uncle Colin and my aunty, and also Aunty Jenny. Nansie had given all the grandkids a gigantic chocolate egg each. There was chocolate everywhere!

When Aunty Jenny came, she brought a big self-made Easter-egg-shaped piñata. Jack had had a great time recently at his cousin Ashley's birthday party with the piñata she had. He'd really looked forward to having a red-hot go at it. The kids all had a go at hitting into the Easter egg piñata, but Jack, oh my goodness, he was smacking into that thing so hard that it fell to the ground. I had not seen so much energy in him for so long. It was a small ray of hope that maybe we still had a chance.

When the piñata hit the floor, Jack continued to lay into it, and finally it cracked. I held up the piñata and shook it while all the lollies came out. The kids ran under it, grabbing as many lollies as they could.

We had an Easter egg hunt and played soccer and other games. It was fantastic to see so much energy in Jack. He truly had a wonderful time. After the morning, we had to give him a well-deserved nap to recover. We all had such a great time over the weekend, and both boys got enough chocolate to last a year.

CHAPTER 31

Saying goodbye to someone we love is never the end. This world is the doorway to our home, a place where we are free from pain and suffering. Our past loved ones continue to be by our side, helping to guide us through our earthly journey until it is our time to return also. There at the doorway of heaven they will greet us and once again we will be together.

On Monday, Jack wanted to go to Nansie's, so she took him for a little while but brought him back not too long after, as he wanted to come home. She told me that he wasn't right and needed pain relief. I gave him what I could, and soon he was acting different. We ended up giving him a dose of seizure medication because he was in a non-responsive state, but it was so hard to judge what to do.

That afternoon, he fell asleep but woke up suddenly. I yelled out to Anthony to help me. Jack started screaming; he had his arms stretched out, and all I remember is his heart piercing screams.

"Help me! Help me!"

We had given him all of the pain medication we were meant to, but he was screaming in agony. We called the hospital for help. They guided us through his medication until he was asleep again and peaceful.

The palliative care team had come to see us throughout this time and helped us with his medication based on how he was tracking. It was good to have someone to call and help us, I had never seen Jack in so much pain before. We had a lot of the family come down to be with us, and later in the afternoon Jack woke up being normal Jack. He wanted to walk but he found it difficult, so I carried him.

He was funny as he joked around with Poppie, saying to him, "Go home, Poppie! Go home!"

I carried Jack out to the lounge room and sat him on me. He wanted some chocolate to eat, and even though he found it hard, we gave him small pieces to melt into his mouth. The family slowly went home, and we put Jack to bed in our bed.

During the night, Jack awoke as he always did, and he sat up onto his knees, still asleep.

"Lay down onto your pillow, buddy," I softly said to him.

"This one?" he asked as he pointed at it.

"Yes," I replied.

He laid himself back down onto the bed and put his head on his pillow. It was then, at this point, that I believe something happened. Jack lay down and then turned facing me and grabbed me around my neck tight, with his little hand cuddling me. This was the last time I would ever hear his beautiful voice again or have his arms wrapped around my neck.

When we awoke the next morning with Jack, it was around four o'clock. This is for me the most difficult moment in my life to write about, and it will be the hardest thing to try to forget. We got Jack up, and the best way to describe it to you, if it is even possible as tears are just flowing down my face, is that he was disabled. He was mentally brain damaged.

He was drooling from the mouth and staring with no emotions, yelling out *"eh! eh! eh!"*

He had to stand up, and he was trying to reach out. We couldn't get him to sit, we just had to hold him up as he tried to walk, moving his legs and reaching out, screaming *"eh!"* We had to put a bib on him, as the amount of saliva drooling from his mouth was uncontrollable.

We had no idea what to do. I called Nansie, and she came over and helped us. She had worked in aged care for many years, and she had seen people dying. She began to explain to me what the final stages of Jack's time here would be like, I got angry and snapped at her. I hated people telling me how it was going to be. So far, the medical professionals had got things wrong. I no longer believed that anything was set in stone.

"Don't you want to know what is going to happen?" Nansie asked.

I replied, "No!"

I needed to deal with the now and the now only! I had enough for now. I could only deal with more as I dealt with it. That's just the kind of person I am. I'd never done anything like this before. I know that Nansie was a nurse and had seen these types of things happen, but for me, I just needed help with now. We called the hospital, they were going to send a nurse to us.

I will never forget those few hours we struggled to hold Jack up and let him try to do what he was doing. He was like a vegetable, completely unable to control himself, what a horrific memory of such a beautiful, intelligent child. It was like he was trying, screaming to just do something that he could easily do before, but his brain and body refused him now. He was trying to tell us that he was still in there, even though he couldn't get out.

The palliative team member knew exactly what to do. Jack was having continual mild seizures, so she gave him something to calm him down to where he still had his eyes open but was not trying to jump about all the time. He sat on my lap, and I held him. He continued to have small seizures where he would grind his teeth and grunt, so the medication was continually adjusted for him. He would have a nap and rest on and off all day while sitting on us in the recliner. We spent most of that night taking turns holding him.

The next night, we decided that we would put Jack into our bed, hoping he would sleep more peacefully, because the previous night we were all a little restless on the recliner. Jack was in our bed, with me lying across the bottom of it holding his hand and Anthony on the floor. Nansie stayed on the couch.

In the morning while Jack was lying in our bed, after a good night's sleep, he heard Joey's voice as she entered through the front door. As soon as he heard her, he lit up somehow and desperately tried to get out of the bed. I picked him up and held him on the recliner in the lounge room, so he could see and hear her close up. Jack loved her so much; his big cousin had always played with him and taken care of him all the time. I can't think of a time they weren't having fun.

Ma had bought four Hot Wheels cars for Jack, Joey unwrapped each one of them slowly in front of him. She described them to him as she placed them up in front of his face, so he could see them, and she then put one in each of his hands. He held on to them tightly.

Throughout these days all our family and friends came and had a chance to hold Jack and talk to him, say goodbye, and thank him for being such a beautiful person.

During this time, I had a very disturbing moment with one of the palliative care nurses when she left in the morning after doing Jack's medications. I looked down at the identification sticker that she had written out and stuck on his medication, she had written "Luke." I freaked out that she had written Luke's name instead of Jack's.

What does that mean? Oh my God, has she condemned Luke? Is this a bad omen?

I yelled to Anthony to come and see, and he was so mad that she had made such a terrible mistake. He crossed out Luke's name so much with a pen that it was just a black pile of ink left on the sticker. It upset me to see Luke's name on that medication. I felt sick in my stomach and found it hard to mentally get rid of it.

Another bloody mistake!

Anthony informed a different nurse who saw Jack later that afternoon, and she could not apologise enough after seeing how much it had upset us. I felt like there was no end to our suffering, that it just had to keep being added to and added to.

How much more could we take?

I still believed. I still naively believed that my wonderful and powerful God could save my son. That night we laid Jack in our bed, and I slept at his feet with Anthony on the floor and Nansie on the couch in the lounge. By this time his medications were tweaked to the right amounts so that there were no more mild seizures, thank God!

The next morning, we washed Jack and redressed him, and his frail little body was so skinny. It was hard seeing him like this—no energy and no life.

Why did this have to take so long? Was he still suffering? Could he still hear us? Feel us?

I continued to rub my nose in Jack's beautiful hair. We decided to leave Jack in our bed from now on during the day instead of having him sit on us on the recliner. We played him Hi-5 music, which was his favourite. We had recently been able to attend their concert, and a few months later, our friends Andy and Sarah contacted the group and were given an amazing box full of merchandise to give to Jack. When they gave it to Jack, it was such a special moment. It really was one of the most special things anyone had ever done for him. What a gift!

We built a big tribute wall around our bed where Jack lay, consisting of as many photos of Jack's life as we could find. We stuck them all over the head of the bed and wall. We then stuck happy-face stickers all over the quilt. He had his new cars and our hands to always hold. We would keep telling him how much we loved him.

Each day had consisted of me constantly checking Jack's heart to see if it was still beating.

Was he still with me?

Jack's breathing had become irregular, and there were large spots of time when Jack would not breathe. The longest we counted was a period of seventy-five seconds. Every time he did it, we just waited, and then he once again took that deep gasping breath.

Luke was just a ball of fun. He thought it was great crawling over Jack and smacking him in the head every now and then. That kid was always doing something to make us laugh. He was our joy in this painful time. He loved Jack so much, and he just wanted to be with him and play like they had always done. He couldn't understand why Jack would not muck around with him. Luke took pride in stealing Jack's food when Jack wasn't looking or messing up Jack's toys. I guess he wanted his big brother to get up and play.

Today, which was Thursday, the garbage man came down the street. Usually Jack would run out and wave to him until the garbage man gave him a *toot toot* with his horn. Jack loved his giant toy garbage trucks Nansie had given him. While Jack lay in our bed slowly dying, my brother Shane ran out to tell the garbage man to toot his horn. Just in the nick of time, he gave out a great big *toot toot!* We couldn't believe it. What a wonderful moment for Jack!

I think every one of our family members was at our house that Thursday evening. They had organised a barbecue, and it was all cooked up and ready to go. Everyone left the room where Jack was to go and have something to eat, but Anthony stayed, and he told me to stay. I continued to look at the picture we had of Mary by Jack's bedside, and in my mind, I begged her to finally give Jack peace and take him. Anthony told me to close the door, so I got up off my knees from the bedside and closed the bedroom door.

"This is it, hurry, hurry!" he said. I was shocked, and I quickly rushed back to Jack's side.

"He's gone!" Anthony said.

"I missed him ..." I said sadly. I couldn't believe that I had missed the moment he passed because I was closing the door.

"No, he had his last breath as you knelt by his side," Anthony reassured me.

I placed my hand onto Jack's heart and waited to feel his tiny heartbeat, but there was nothing. He was gone. He lay there staring into Anthony's eyes as Anthony knelt by his side. How beautiful that he was looking into his daddy's eyes as he left us.

I looked up towards the sky and said, "Goodbye, Jack, I love you!" and Anthony said it too.

Anthony slowly closed Jack's eyes, and then we positioned him in the middle of the bed with his arms and legs straight and his eyes closed. Our little boy was gone. He had gone home to heaven.

For some reason, I had believed that there would be something wonderful that would happen when Jack passed. That I would see or hear something profound, a light, a song, a singing angel, I don't know, just something. But there was nothing. I was a little saddened about not being focused on Jack and truly seeing him when he died, but Anthony was there, and he knew that it was Jack's time to go. We walked out to the family room where everyone was getting food.

Anthony slowly said to them, "He's gone."

"What? He's gone?" Nansie rushed to see him.

They all couldn't believe it. They were only just with him a moment ago. The time was around six fifteen Thursday evening, April 16. Anthony said that Jack would have passed around six thirteen, but I decided that he passed at six fifteen, as I now hated the number thirteen. We lived at number thirteen and look what had happened here.

We all sat and stood around Jack in the bedroom where he lay peacefully. There was a knock at the door, and it was our good friends Sarah and Andy with food they had made. They had come just moments after Jack's passing. They entered into our bedroom where he lay peacefully, surrounded by all those that loved him, and they said goodbye. He was gone. My Jack was gone. The numbness had returned where there were no feelings. In a way, I was happy for Jack, that he was now free of such pain and agony.

Unknown to me, Anthony had already arranged with Uncle Colin the details of collecting Jack. Uncle Colin knew someone who worked with him in the police force who now owned a funeral business. Anthony called Uncle Colin, and he asked his funeral director friend to come out to the house after explaining our situation. We were given the opportunity to let Jack stay in the bed with us during the night, but he had gone. My beautiful Jack's soul had gone, and so I did not want to keep him lying there all night, empty and motionless.

Nansie had rushed home and collected flowers from her garden. She made a long pathway of flowers from our front door to the funeral car. Anthony and I had a moment by ourselves to say one final goodbye to our beautiful Jack. I rubbed my nose in his hair as much as I could, just to feel his soft beautiful hair on my skin for the last time. I removed a piece of his hair with some scissors, so I could keep it forever.

When we were finished, Anthony gently lifted Jack from our bed and placed him onto the stretcher the funeral parlour had provided us. The funeral director slowly zipped up the black body bag over Jack's lifeless body and then his face. They wheeled Jack's covered body through the house and out the front door and down the walkway where Nansie had placed the beautiful flowers from her garden along the path on both sides as a tribute to Jack. He had loved Nansie's garden.

As the funeral director opened the back of his van to place Jack into its hollow, dark emptiness, a few balloons were quickly placed in there with him. It was a comfort for us all to know that there was some colour and something that gave Jack so much joy in his life.

When Jack was driven away, we were left not knowing what to do. I mean, what do you do? My brother Shane hugged me, saying, "I've lost my best friend!"

We sat down and played our home movies of Jack and decided to spend the night remembering him and just laughing at the things he used to do. I will never forget the time when Jack had a craft set out with small fluffy balls that you could stick on rocks to make a nose on your rock friends. There were large, medium, and small ones of these fluffy balls. For some reason, Jack wanted to sniff them, and so he sniffed a large one. He then proceeded to sniff a small one, and wouldn't you know, it shot straight up his nostril! He started screaming, but all I had to do was close his other nostril and tell him to blow it out, and he did. I tried so hard not to laugh, but to this day it just cracks me up.

Man, I just love you, Jack! We love you, Jack!

I went to my top drawer in my bedroom for some reason and found the plastic bag that had Jack's T-shirt in it from his original operation. I opened it to see what was on it. To my surprise, it was a plane, the only form of transport he had not been on, and the writing on the shirt said, "Just flying by." How true that small phrase was. In some small way, it comforted me at that very moment, as if he had left it behind especially for me to find.

Thank you, Jack!

I couldn't sleep on the side of the bed where Jack had passed. It was all really weird, not knowing where he was. Could he see us? Was he somewhere else? Was he home in heaven? I hoped that he was home in heaven in the arms of his maker smiling down upon us.

Oh God, how I miss you already!

CHAPTER 32

See the signs of communication between our world and the next.
The angels who are talking to us use subtle ways to help guide us
throughout our lives. Listen and hear their voices through songs
and poems. See their help through images and items. They are
always communicating to us.

Over the next few days, we organised Jack's funeral. Anthony and I didn't think about any expense, we just planned it to how we knew Jack would love it. We picked a spot in the cemetery park in the children's section that was behind Daisy, who was the only child there in this row.

"Is she your friend, Jack?" I would ask him. I could imagine him running around in the grass holding her hand.

"Oh, she's your girlfriend, is she?"

For some reason, it made me feel at peace that she was there, and she had been all alone, and now Jack would be there with her to keep her company.

The funeral was planned for Tuesday, which made me at ease, as the Monday was Anthony's and my wedding anniversary. We didn't want Jack's funeral on the same day as that. We organised a handsome white suit for Jack to wear and wanted beautiful colourful balloons in the ceremony room, Jack loved balloons. We chose all the beautiful songs and poems that we needed throughout the funeral and a range of photos that would be displayed of Jack.

I was a little scared after Jack passed because I had thought that there would be a beautiful light or a loving feeling or something, but it never happened. The thought of nothing after we die is scary.

A few days after Jack passed, I asked him, "How will I know if you are okay, Jack?"

His favourite colour was pink, and we had decided on pink and white flowers for the funeral, but although I dislike the colour yellow, I loved yellow roses. They were my favourite.

So, I said to Jack, "I would like you to give me a yellow rose to show me that you are okay." I just needed to know that he was at peace.

The day I was choosing the photos for the funeral, I was struck down by a photo of Jack. He was sitting on Nansie's grass in her garden holding a massive yellow rose up as if giving it to the person looking at the photo. There it was: my yellow rose. It was even given to me by Jack himself. I don't remember Nansie having roses in her garden, and it was yellow, exactly what I had asked for. Even the expression on his face was like he had planned it all before he passed because he knew I would ask for it. I was blown away, and now I knew he was safe and happy.

We had a private viewing of Jack at the funeral director's premises before we went to the cemetery for the funeral, where we saw Jack in his coffin wearing his beautiful white suit. It was Anthony's immediate family and mine and our friends Jenny, Sarah, and Andy who were there. Jack looked different, though. It wasn't the Jack I remembered. He was still beautiful, and I loved to once again be able to rub my nose in his beautiful blonde hair. But this body I was looking at was only the shell of Jack that he used to walk this earth with, and that is exactly what it looked like, a lifeless shell. The real Jack was in heaven.

Many of us placed things inside the coffin that Jack had loved so much in his life, like toys, chocolate frogs, and cars. It was nice to think that we had put them in there for him. This was a strange time. I would cry a lot, but there was still only a great numbness to me. It was my mind and my body trying to shelter and protect me from the truth of the situation.

Luke was looking extremely handsome in his little suit with a pink flower on his chest. We had stated in the funeral notices that Jack loved the colour pink, and so we all wore something pink. I chose a pink shirt to wear, and Anthony had a pink tie. We arrived at the funeral a little early, as we wanted to see the room set up. There were these amazingly beautiful bright balloons standing tall on either side of the room. I immediately cried, because the colours were so rich and perfect. Jack would have loved them.

There were already flowers that had been sent by people we knew, and I knelt down and read all the cards. Soon people were arriving, and I tried my best to be strong, which I was, because I still felt numb all over. Anthony and I tried to acknowledge everyone who was there.

The ceremony started, and as Anthony, my brother Shane, Anthony's brother Brenton, and our friend Andy carried Jack's coffin down the aisle, something strange happened. As soon as they passed Luke asleep in his pram, he woke in fright screaming. I picked him up and held him tight, but he was inconsolable for about five minutes. He knew his brother was gone, and he was sad.

The rest of the ceremony was beautiful. The photos of Jack were funny and sad. Uncle Colin stood up and read all of the messages that we had written to Jack to say goodbye. Nansie had purchased and wrapped a Matchbox car for each of the kids who had come and played with Jack throughout his life, his friends. It was a final gift from Jack to his friends who he loved so much. Anthony and I handed them out as we called out each of their names, which was beautiful. I'm so glad that she thought of doing that.

Our neighbour's daughter from across the road, Kate, was called up. She was only a one-year-old when we moved into our family home, and she had grown up in front of our eyes. Kate was now thirteen; she had seen Jack through it all and loved him so very much. All our neighbours had supported us well throughout our whole time with Jack. We were very lucky. Kate was the oldest of all of Jack's friends, and so we gave her two cars to remember him by.

I made sure that I soaked in every moment, every photo, and every song throughout the ceremony so that I would never forget. We walked behind Jack's coffin to his gravesite, where everyone had the chance to throw a flower over him. We handed each of the children one of the coloured helium balloons. Nansie was holding Luke, so she shared an orange balloon with him. They all let the balloons go together so the balloons could rise up to Jack in heaven.

One of my friends from work, Bek, had brought me two pink stone hearts. One was bigger, which represented my heart, and one was smaller, which represented Jack's. We placed the bigger heart on top of Jack's coffin to symbolise that my heart was always with him, and I kept the smaller heart, which meant that his heart was always with me. It was beautiful to know that we had done that.

The day slowly passed, and the funeral was perfect for Jack. He would have loved it. Everything about the funeral had been perfect, and I was over the moon with how much effort and love had gone into it to make it so personalised for Jack. This was his goodbye, and this was my final time to say to him that I would miss him and let him go home.

I love you, my beautiful son. Jack, to me you are a hero and an angel. You are my inspiration in my life and I will shine your love upon this world for as long as I live.

At home on the Thursday, one week after Jack had passed, I could hear the garbage man coming down the road. I went into Jack's bedroom window and stood there watching as he collected the garbage. To my surprise, he let out a great big *toot toot!* I actually jumped a little and raised my hand to wave and say thank you. The surprise of it was too much, and as I turned, I could not hold in all my tears. I will never forget it. Maybe that was Jack's way of saying hi, I just don't know, but the garbage man never ever did it again.

I decided soon after to pack up Jack's room. I don't know why I decided to do it so quickly. The only thing I can come up with is that I was still numb. I had no feeling, and so it really was the best time to do it. It was hard, but I felt like I was doing the right thing at the time. I packed the things I wanted to keep in containers and slowly sorted through them.

The time drew closer when we needed to pay for the funeral. There was $1,200 left for us to pay. It was scary, because although the funeral was perfect, it was time now to come up with the funds to pay for it. We had used so much money throughout the year and we did not have the money right now. The children's cancer charity we were connected to and another charity had donated a great sum of money to go towards the funeral, which was amazing and greatly appreciated, we were still in need of the remaining $1,200. There was also the headstone to be put up for Jack at the gravesite but there was plenty of time to save up for that, and it wasn't a bill.

Anthony was finding it stressful with everything that was going on, and with this extra financial pressure put on him. He decided to have a drink at the pub to just chill out by himself. He bought a beer and drank it. Then he bought another one and walked over to the pokies room and sat down with his fifty dollars. There he asked Jack to help us. He pressed the button over and over and watched the money slowly run down. His heart sank ... until he heard singing. It wasn't in his head, it was the pokie machine singing! He couldn't believe it. He had won!

He stood there staring at the machine and thought *maybe I could win a bit more*, but this little soft voice in his head said, "Daddy, it's time to leave now." And so, he did.

He came home a little freaked out as he pulled $1,200 from his wallet, the exact amount we had left to pay off the funeral. The exact amount! I guess it is okay to ask for help when you need it.

Thanks, Jack, our angel.

There continued to be small weird happenings around us. One day when I did the dishes, I went to wipe over the sink when I had finished. I noticed some suds in the ridges of the sink in one corner. As I went to wipe them away, I stopped and noticed that they spelt out the word "HI" perfectly. I took a photo because it was so weird. The suds had formed a perfect H and a perfect I.

So, I just looked up to the heavens and said, "Hi, Jack."

Every time now we see a butterfly fly around us, we say hello to Jack. I know that he is watching over us and the butterfly is such a beautiful peaceful creature that represents new life. Even Luke says hello to the butterflies now and yells "Jack!" I love that he does that. It acknowledges Jack's life and that we will always remember him.

So now I decided that one day this book would be written. I wanted to acknowledge Jack's life. Even though my memories of all these events were still fresh in my mind, I knew that one day they wouldn't be. I wondered if it was possible to somehow get a hold of Jack's hospital records so that I would know precisely the dates and cycles of Jack's chemotherapy and everything else that had happened with him at the hospital.

Nansie rang me one day out of the blue and told me that she had spoken to Uncle Colin and he said all I had to do was go up to the records counter at the hospital and request a form to apply for a copy of all of Jack's records.

Could it actually be that simple? I wondered.

So, one day Nansie, Poppie, Luke, and I went for a day out. While Nansie and Poppie played with Luke in the park opposite the specialist hospital, I walked in the front door, went straight to the counter, asked for the form, and walked out. It was that simple! Hmm, well, it wasn't quite that simple. The whole time I was there (all of five minutes) I felt like I was this enemy! I felt like I was on some detective mission and was secretly entering the enemy's barracks and obtaining information that was top secret and forbidden to be released.

Why did I feel this way? This was a whole chapter of my son's life ... it was his life! And I was his mother, and technically it belonged to me. That's how I saw it, anyway. The lady at the counter who handed me the form explained to me what to do, but she did not hide her thoughts well. I could tell that she was looking at me sideways and wondering why I wanted such valuable information. I felt like I was walking on eggshells, because who goes out and requests medical records?

Anyway, I did it, and man, it was one of the hardest things I've ever had to do, but it was the most empowering. I felt like for the first time I had a choice and I took it. I went over and met Nansie and Poppie at the park and told them how easy it was to obtain the form.

Luke was playing with a large pine cone that he wanted to take home, Nansie took a photo of Luke and me with his pine cone.

I said, "This pine cone will mark the day that we went in and started the process of obtaining Jack's medical records and the beginning of the book I will write of Jack's story." I went home and filled out that form, and I sent it in.

A few weeks later, the package arrived in the post, and it was huge. I organised it neatly in some plastic sleeves in a large folder and read through it slowly so that I could understand the order of it and read all the comments from the doctors. It was interesting, I must say! I happily read over the comments of that horrible day that Jack was never meant to recover from, knowing that they were completely wrong. I discovered the paracetamol overdose in the ICU when he had his initial brain operation. The comments calling him a "Psycho child" when he was on certain medications. Interesting, very interesting.

So, there it was, Jack's bible of his hospital life and my platform for writing this book. It made my job easier to remember the order of facts and the events that happened. Everything was there, in black and white, and so the book was started.

One year later, on the anniversary of Jack's death, we had a big day of remembering. We decided that every year we would send balloons to heaven for Jack at the gravesite, all of us having the same colours as we did on the day of his funeral. We would eat all the foods that Jack loved to eat, like donuts, chocolate frogs, pasties, ham sandwiches, veggie chips, and of course Nansie's chocolate cakes. At six fifteen that evening, we drank milk from Easter eggs and did cheers with them in honour of Jack's life. Nansie today had also released a tribute to Jack for his one-year anniversary within the local Catholic paper. It was a wonderful way of remembering him at this time, but it was still hard for us to cope with, not just losing him but the memories of the pain and suffering he had endured.

At around eleven o'clock that night, when everyone was in bed, Aunty Jenny and I sat on the couch reminiscing, talking about the day and telling 'Jack' stories. Suddenly, the earth began to shake. Yes, the earth began to shake. I was absolutely shocked that where we lived had even had an earthquake. It wasn't massive, but it was enough for us to wonder what on earth was happening.

Jenny turned on the radio to hear the confirmation that we had just had an earthquake, and for some reason I was comforted. My heart was breaking from the loss of my son, and the earth had shaken in agony for me. But it wasn't scary or sad. Instead, it was powerful, like I was shown by God himself that he felt my pain, and I was thankful for his acknowledgement of it. Jack was always with me, and this confirmed it. I went to bed as I did every night clasping the rosary beads that Nansie had placed in Jack's hands while he slipped away from us, and I remembered him.

For some reason, for the first few years after Jack passed, I found it easy to talk about him with others, even though I could see that others found it hard for me to talk about him. This book had been started and was on its way, and I knew that it would be a very slow process, but you know what? Jack would show me signs that this was how it was meant to be.

There would be times when I gave myself a beating over how long it was taking me to write. But today I know that it could never have been written any faster than what it was. I would receive small hints that would encourage me to remember to write, and I could never write when others were around. Most of this book was written through blurry, tear-filled eyes, but there was no other way. I hope that I have told your story, dear Jack, with the passion it deserves.

I love you!

CHAPTER 33

The enemy has knocked me down, dragged me through the dirt, stomped on me, beaten me, and torn at my heart. He turns and walks away laughing at me and decides to look over his shoulder at my broken shell one more time ... but as he turns, he sees that I am standing tall and pointing my right hand towards the skies. I look deep into his eyes and I say to him, "I am still here, and you will never *defeat me!" As light pours from the heavens, blinding the enemy, he runs in fear, knowing that I am more powerful than he can ever be.*

It's been a while now, since Jack's passing, and I still miss his beautiful presence every single minute of every day. There will never be a moment for me that does not have a thought of him within it. How does any mother get through such suffering? My life has changed forever, and it will never be the same again.

Throughout the years after losing Jack, there has been a long journey of recovery for me to the place where I am right now. Sometimes you have to fall before you are able to spread your wings and fly.

A few years ago, about three years after Jack's passing, I found myself in a whirlwind of even more agony. Somehow, I was in a place where I was just a shell of the person I had once been. I was alone, suffering in silence, and allowing the grief and the heartache to consume my very existence. But surely, I was allowed to do this?

Every day seemed like a struggle until it came to the point where the small duties that were normal each day would become too much to bear. I had come to terms with the loss of my eldest son. I was sure that I had.

Hadn't I?

But for some reason, my body was starting to fail me. I do not know to this day where I would be if it were not for my beautiful son, Luke, and my amazing husband, Anthony, still here upon this earth and loving me completely. The feeling of being torn was a daily occurrence, which created a fight inside of me, a battle of where my mind should wander. Sometimes I just wanted to sit and think about the memories of Jack without any disturbance ... or should I be laughing and playing with Luke? After what I had been through, shouldn't I be soaking up every single moment I had with Luke instead of wondering about Jack?

Society began to play with me like a toy, and the numbness I had felt inside for so long decided to disappear, leaving my emotions to rage as if turned on full blast within my aching soul. As Luke grew up, he began kindergarten, and his life making friends started to bloom. What also began were the taunts from within my mind, which started to continuously attack me.

Why? Why? Why? Why did this happen to us? It's just not fair!

This would play over and over, somehow trying to find an answer to a question that was unanswerable. Just speaking Jack's name had suddenly became too much. Life was fine when my feelings were numb. Back then I felt strong when talking about Jack even when others did not. But my body had finally decided that I had to face the truth, to remember the pain.

My anger would rage at the hospital sometimes to the point where I would wonder about taking legal action. Surely someone should be held accountable. But deep down, I had always known that Jack's life had to be remembered in a positive way. I knew that although mistakes had been made throughout Jack's treatment, everyone involved had done the best they could with the knowledge they had at the time.

I couldn't let my anger overtake who I was and who I remembered Jack to be. His life story, I hope, will change the world, and so nothing, definitely not money, would change the way things were. It wouldn't bring me peace, and it wouldn't ease my pain. Instead, it would be a Band-Aid that eventually would need to be torn off, revealing a wound that still bled. What dollar figure could stop this pain?

None.

Luke continued to grow and then started school. He had become such an amazing boy. I watched as other mothers picked up their children in Luke's year. As they carried a younger sibling within their arms or awaited the older sibling to catch up to them as they collected their much-loved family at school pick up. Although the thoughts were deep inside of my mind, they were still there.

Why is it that all of these people were allowed to keep their children? Why was my Jack taken?

Of course, I never wanted anything bad for anyone, it was just a question of why me and why Jack out of so many normal families. Had I done something wrong? As I gazed upon these families with jealousy, I realised that I always noticed when the mothers would tell their kids off or speak down to them.

All I could think was, *Do you truly know how lucky you are just to have them?*

As friends began announcing their pregnancies and the next addition to their families, excited about their second, third, or even fourth precious cargo, I felt robbed. I knew that my body could not endure another pregnancy, and neither could my mind. Maybe if I had started younger, I could have had more children.

Was it all right for me to not be happy for them? It was like a knife piercing my heart every single time. I didn't want to feel this way. I truly loved the fact that my friends and family were having more additions. It was that small little voice that would play on me. The initial reaction would be pure happiness, and then when I was alone it was a crushing sadness.

I remember the advice of people who tried to help when Luke was emotional at school because he was unsure of the unknown. Their voices would echo over and over.

"Don't worry, Luke's just like that because he's an only child!"

I knew why Luke was emotional and scared of the things he was unsure about. He had not only felt my fear within my womb, but he had also seen his brother pass. Oh, how I wanted to yell at these people and tell them that it wasn't Luke's fault that he didn't have a brother. But I didn't, because these normal people did not know anything about us. Why should I tell them anyway? It would just make them feel bad, and it would make me remember my own pain.

"Are you going to have more children? Luke will be lonely if you don't!" people would tease.

I knew that everyone meant well, and people were trying to be funny. Little did they know the loss I had already endured. Their comical words would continue to remind me of that.

As time passed and the list of doctors I had visited grew, I realised that there must be an answer to all of my whys, not just for me but for Jack also. I had received no real diagnosis from the mounting number of symptoms I was now facing on a daily basis. I found myself at that point where many say you are at your lowest of lows, but I seemed to just keep falling. There came a point in my life when I suddenly realised that the situation I was in was not going to get better. I was continuing on a path that had no good outcome, and so the question I posed to myself was... *Am I worth it?*

The question wasn't whether or not my beautiful son Luke or my amazing husband Anthony were worth it. No, it was, am I worth it? Am

I worth the time and the effort it would take to understand all of the whys that I was asking? Was it worth the pain and suffering it would cause to be able to heal? Was I worth healing? These were hard questions to answer, because the road to recovery and happiness appeared to be so long, exhausting and out of reach.

Many would agree that it was just too much to even comprehend, let alone face and accomplish. When you are running on empty already, it's hard to commit to something more. But I chose to answer this question with a small yes.

Yes, I am worth it!

How could I not be? I wanted to be the person I had always been, and I wanted to be that person for my family also. Luke needed a mother who could support him in every way, and Anthony a wife who could do the same. But this had to be about me. Finally, I acknowledged that I had always put everything else first. Everything else had come before the decision to take care of myself. I had come to a place where if I didn't start taking care of myself, there would be no more Tarina left to worry about. Then who would take care of Luke? Who would take care of Anthony?

Why do we have to lose so much within our lives before we finally choose to change? I had lost my eldest son to cancer, and now I was losing my body to the emotional backlash of grief. Something had to change.

The next few years for me were full of change, a very, very slow change. I realised that I didn't have to have the perfect outcome within a single moment. Instead, I prepared for the journey. I chose not to focus on a final product of who I wanted to be. I read, watched, attended, listened, and tried every single thing I could that would somehow answer all the questions as to why my life was the way it was.

I have learned so much and become so much more. There were so many doors closed, and yet so many opened. There were things I didn't agree with, and things that enlightened my soul. Not everything I did was progressive, but I realised that no matter what information I extracted from the world, I would get something from it, no matter how small. If it made me feel good, I embraced it.

To get through my journey of grief, I had to accept that I needed to take ownership of it and allow it. I was allowed to feel; that was my right, and I was allowed to experience it in any way that was right for me. No matter what others would say, I learned to listen to myself and my inner guidance.

Why are we always so damn worried about what other people think about us? I was scared to cry, scared to release all the tension, especially in front of people, because of what they might think. The one thing that Jack taught me was to have courage. So now I had to realise that other people's thoughts are no longer my business. Why was I playing a game of what-if? I'm not a psychic, so why was I trying so hard to be one, continuously imagining what someone was thinking about me and wondering if they were judging me?

I was even playing out scenarios in my head about what people would be saying to other people, how they would be spreading horrible rumours. The most amazing thing anyone can do for their own well-being is to stop playing out these pointless scenarios that will never ever be true. What a waste of time! What a waste of life! Stop doing it and see how freeing that is.

As I read every book, attended every seminar, and watched every interview about life and death that I could find, I discovered many, many amazing things. But the one thing that was most amazing of all that I discovered was ... me.

All along, all I was really trying to find was me, the real me, my truth. The biggest question most of us want answered is, who am I?

Over five years, I collated so much information from the outside world: from scientists, doctors, gurus, spiritual leaders, and people who had near-death experiences, etc. But after all those years of slowly step-by-step recreating myself, I realised that no matter how much information and knowledge I attained from the outside world, all I really needed to do was look within. I already had all the answers. I had just become so disconnected from them and from myself because of the events that had occurred within my whole life, my entire life. It wasn't just about Jack; it was about every single thing I had decided to take on board throughout my whole existence.

I remembered moments within my life that had caused such a huge impact that it controlled many of the decisions I had been making. Let me share with you one of those stories.

Everyone has felt the wrath and the pain caused by another human being's words or their actions, right? Those things that hurt us then cause judgement from ourselves, creating a choice that we make that allows us to believe we are somehow tainted. We believe that we are imperfect. We choose to become not good enough.

My ego got a bruising at around the age of ten years old. A friend of my mother told her that I would be nothing more than a checkout chick (a supermarket operator). The way it was intended was that there was no worth to that position (which is of course not true) and that I could become no more within my life. That comment and the way it was intended really hurt!

When I graduated from school at the age of sixteen, that is exactly the job I applied for, a checkout chick. This decision was made easier when my mother came home with the application form from a local supermarket. Within my mind it confirmed that my mother indeed believed that horrible statement told to me at the age of ten, that I would be nothing more than a checkout chick. The decisions I made in my career path were based on that one woman's comment and information that probably was all completely made up in my head. These choices kept me within the retail industry of food and clothing for the whole of my working career.

Why? Because I was told that I wasn't good enough to do anything else.

Did I love the jobs I had chosen? Well, there have been some really great moments, and I have met many awesome people, but did I love what I was doing? No.

So, my question is, how could one person's single comment to me when I was ten years old become the basis of all of my career decisions throughout my entire lifetime? It dragged me through a career I didn't really love, and it made me turn my head away from all of the creative ideas that had been sprouting within my mind since the age of five.

It had become easier for me to blame that friend of my mother for all of those years of choices I had made than to actually do something about it.

Why? Because I might have failed.

Which then would make my mother's friend right, not to mention the fact that this also gave me an excuse and someone to blame for my lack of effort. If I did actually try doing something that I loved and failed, then I would have no dream to never reach. Correct?

Here's the thing. It wasn't my mother's friend's fault, was it? It was mine! I was the one who allowed her voice to become belief within my soul instead of really going out there and doing what I loved and being true to myself. I look at it now and I can't believe it. How could I have done this to myself for so long? Had I been blinded by the power of those words, allowing that one moment to somehow take control of me? This woman was just one person in my life, just one experience. How many other moments had I allowed to affect me and the choices I had been making? I finally gave myself permission to shine and to start that journey of becoming who I had always wanted to be. How exciting!

Maybe, just maybe, Jack's short life was all about teaching me how to find myself, to find who I really was. There is not one life within this world that does not have purpose, not one. I learned to believe in myself and to create my own beliefs instead of dragging around the useless old ones that in no way served me or had any meaning to me anymore. There were many times I would read a book or watch an interview and have a light bulb moment. Many of these moments would draw me back to Jack, as if he himself had planted small pieces of information like crumbs for me to find.

I learned that Jack was teaching me about me. He always had been, even when he was here. It just took me some time to understand it. Jack was giving me the courage that he had shown me when he was alive. He never gave up, and he never complained. It was my turn now to pass that on.

I finally believe that Jack really is okay and that he is with me always. There is always that doubt when you lose someone, but now there is only peace in my heart...not just for Jack, but for all of us. The fear of death can consume us, becoming the very thing that makes us sick in the first place. I am learning to let it go. I am not a doctor, I am not a scientist, and I am definitely not a therapist, but I have healed, and I continue to heal every single day.

Why? Because I choose to, and because I allow myself to.

That means getting out of my own way. I give confusion to a higher power and let it go. Amazing things happen when you do this, amazing!

Life for me is a journey, and I have chosen to be awake and a part of it instead of allowing myself to hide within it. I no longer believe in rejection and failure. I no longer believe that I am limitless. I was born perfect, and I will always be perfect. I am running my own race and living the life that I want, doing things that make me happy and bring me joy.

Jack only ever did what made him happy. He played and had fun no matter how he felt. Why shouldn't I do that too? I have always wanted to create, to write books, and now I believe that I can. Jack has taught me that life is short, and now is the time to get up and do all of those amazing things I have always wanted to do but have been too scared to.

My choices now come from love and not fear. I embrace every single part of me, even the scary bits. We all have those! But like I said, I will embrace them without judgement. I'm still human, and I still get angry, which is just fine, as long as I don't hold onto it and allow it to consume me. I will love myself because that is the most important thing that I can ever do. Loving myself will save my life. Love is truly all there is.

Here is a story that I find fits appropriately. It's a story that happened while I was with my beautiful Jack.

One night I was getting ready to go out and have dinner with a couple of my girlfriends. Even though it was hard to feel the urge to actually want to try to make myself look somewhat decent, I finally accepted the fact that there wasn't much else I could do. I had put a small amount of makeup on and put on something nice that fitted, even though I felt like a giant fat elephant.

As I walked out to the front of the lounge, I saw Jack's face from where he was eating his dinner on his little blue table and chairs, which faced the television and now me. Jack's eyes instantly lit up as his mouth slowly opened. He leaned backwards in his chair as if gravity itself had pushed him back, and without any hesitation he spoke these words to me, "Mummy, you look beautiful!"

I saw the reaction, the beautiful face my three-year-old little boy had just given me, and it was the undeniably instant truth of how he saw me within that moment. It blew me away!

Although I had voices in my head telling me that I had no energy, that there was no need to look good because it wasn't at all possible, and I had the torture of knowing how overweight I was, all of that instantly evaporated. The truth was not what was going on inside of my head but inside the eyes and words of an innocent and judgeless three-year-old little boy. I was a completely different person that night because I believed and knew that I was beautiful and nothing else mattered.

This is what I want you to understand from this story. It is you who creates the negative concepts within your own mind. It is your own made-up perceptions. Change your thoughts and become more. We are all beautiful, and we are all perfect beings on our own journeys.

Even though I will admit that the beautiful state of mind Jack gave me that night was short-lived, I now realised that unique moment will stick with me for all the days of my life. It caused such a strong and beautiful emotion of pure love that had now engrained itself within my memory forever. I can now honestly see, after all of this time and returning to the memory of this moment, how beautiful I have always been.

I had, in the past, continually tortured myself for not being good enough. But not good enough for who? Why can't we just allow ourselves to shine instead of continuously being afraid of it.

I leave you with this. I leave you with love, joy, and gratitude, and I tell you that no matter what you may be going through in your life, you are completely loved, and you are worth it. You are worth the effort to be everything you were created to be.

My life is an amazing and unbelievable journey that continues to unfold every day, and as the sun rises I await its adventures. Life is about experience, and that means experiencing not just perfect happiness but all of life, everything. The ups and the downs. You cannot know who you are, or who you want to be, until you have known who you do not want to be.

I have chosen to create a world that shines light and love, knowing that when things get a little tough, I'm allowed to feel whatever I naturally feel. I do this without any judgement, because it's my experience, and then I let it go, giving it to something greater than myself. I love myself for who I am. Jack has finally taught me to live fearlessly, to do what I enjoy, and to never be afraid of my light.

I no longer separate my world. I choose not to do everything with the intention of getting what I want from it; I choose the intention of giving the world all that I am and all that I was created to be. I will shine my light as gloriously and as brightly as I can with joy, and I will only do what gives me happiness. Together we will create an amazing world. I will accept my journey as my journey and enjoy every moment of it. I will enjoy the present moment because no other time exists. Living in the past or worrying about the future will take you out of the now.

Jack has taught me so many powerful lessons, but his greatest lesson of all is, you are what you believe. Jack never doubted me. He never judged me. He believed in me. I choose to follow his wisdom and to give myself the greatest gift that I can: I will believe. I have seen amazing things happen within my life because I have believed completely. Now I choose to be the best me that I can be.

I choose what I believe in.

I choose what voice I listen to.

I choose to be aware.

I choose which energy I send out into the world.

I choose what I create.

I choose the life I want.

I choose to love myself.

I choose to forgive myself.

I choose to love you.

I choose to forgive you.

My gift to you is to tell you that you can live life to the fullest knowing that living involves experiencing, so get out there and experience everything that you can. Focus on your dreams and do it. Why not? Be grateful and remember that love is all there is, so start loving yourself and the world. Give every creation within this beautiful world of ours the respect it deserves and love every moment you are breathing. It is a gift!

You are what you believe, so remember all you need to do is...

22-months-old

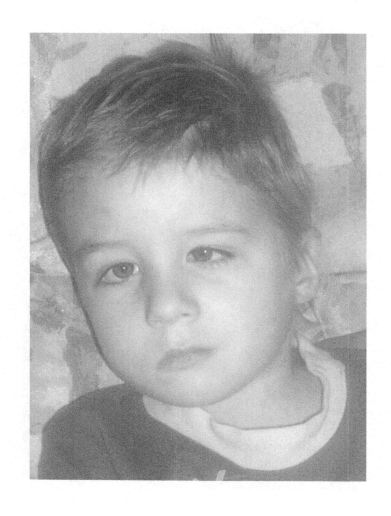

3-and-a-half-years-old

REVIEWS

Thank you for being a part of this journey with us.
It would be greatly appreciated if you could take the time to leave an honest
review about the book.

Amazon:
https://books2read.com/u/bzgWQq
Goodreads:
https://www.goodreads.com/tarinamarcinkowski
Thank you!

ABOUT THE AUTHOR

Tarina Marcinkowski
(Also writes children's books under Jackie Lukes), Is a mother of two, her eldest son Jack is an angel in heaven, and her youngest son Luke is her inspiration that encourages her to write and create every day. Together with her husband and youngest son they all live happily in Adelaide, Australia.

The authors first book 'Just Believe' is the story about her eldest son Jack who passed away from brain cancer. This book is Jack's journey told through the authors eyes as his mother. From this painful experience grew the authors strength to follow her passion of writing and illustrating.

Delving into many different genres including fiction, the author also creates children's books under the pseudonym of Jackie Lukes. This author is a true Australian inspiration.

Follow the Author

Website:

https://tarinamarcinkowski.com

Amazon:

https://www.amazon.com/author/tarinamarcinkowski

Goodreads:

https://www.goodreads.com/tarinamarcinkowski

Facebook:

https://www.facebook.com/tarinamarcinkowski/

Instagram:

https://www.instagram.com/tarina.m.author/

TikTok:

https://vm.tiktok.com/ZSJs99C5R/

CONTINUE THE JOURNEY...

**When Life Chews You Up
and Spits You Out... Eat Chocolate!**
A Guide to Surviving Being Human: Book One

Surviving the everyday trials of being human requires chocolate.
Written by a mother who survived crippling grief after the loss of her young son. This inspirational book uses the authors love of chocolate as a light-hearted way to share her darkest thoughts, deepest emotions, and disabling pain through the... 30 different sessions with chocolate.
A sequel to the memoir, Just Believe: Jack's Inspirational True Story Told Through His Mothers Eyes, this books purpose is to bring hope to those suffering from loss.
Tarina's transformation from one of heartache to joy, is unravelled as she shares her personal journey towards discovering the truth; that life doesn't have to be an everyday struggle. Anyone can be happy and change their life for the better. All they need is the right tools and the right fuel.
So, go out there and have fun, live life to the fullest without giving up all the good stuff... like chocolate.
Chocolate is awesome, and life is meant to be lived!

https://books2read.com/u/bz1wVn

Made in United States
Orlando, FL
24 April 2023